AI for Everyone: A Step-by-Step Guide for Seniors

Josiah Wolff

Published by Josiah Wolff, 2024.

AI FOR EVERYONE: A STEP-BY-STEP GUIDE FOR SENIORS

First edition. September 20, 2024.

Copyright © 2024 Josiah Wolff.

ISBN: 979-8227212580

Written by Josiah Wolff.

Table of Contents

AI for Everyone: A Step-by-Step Guide for Seniors

To my beloved wife, for your endless patience, support, and understanding throughout this journey. Your love made this book possible. Thank you.

Chapter 1: Welcome to the World of AI

What is AI and Why Should You Care?

Welcome to the exciting world of Artificial Intelligence, or AI for short. You might have heard the term thrown around in the news, on your phone, or from friends and family, but what exactly is AI, and why should it matter to you?

Simply put, AI is when machines or computers learn to do tasks that would normally require human intelligence. These tasks could include recognizing faces in photos, understanding speech, answering questions, or even playing a game of chess. But don't worry—AI isn't as complicated as it sounds! In fact, you've probably already used it without even knowing.

AI in Your Everyday Life

Let's start by talking about where AI shows up in your life. You may not realize it, but AI is already helping you in more ways than you think. Here are a few examples:

- **Voice Assistants** like Siri, Google Assistant, or Alexa are all powered by AI. When you ask them to set a reminder or play your favorite song, they're using AI to understand your request and respond in the best way possible.
- **Smartphone Cameras** use AI to make your photos look better by automatically adjusting lighting or focusing on the right parts of an image.
- **Email Services** use AI to help organize your inbox by filtering out spam or suggesting quick replies to messages.
- **Streaming Services** like Netflix or YouTube use AI to recommend shows and videos you might like, based on what you've watched before.

These are just a few ways AI is already making everyday tasks simpler and more efficient. The best part? You don't need to be a tech expert to benefit from it.

How AI Can Make Your Life Easier

Now that you know where AI is, let's talk about how it can make your life easier. AI is designed to help you with tasks that might take too long, be too confusing, or that you simply don't want to do yourself. Here are a few real-life scenarios where AI can step in:

- **Getting Directions**: If you've ever used Google Maps or a GPS system in your car, you've used AI. It helps you find the fastest route, avoid traffic, and even tells you where to turn.
- **Shopping Online**: When you shop on websites like Amazon, AI helps by suggesting products based on what you've bought before, saving you time searching for what you need.
- **Staying Healthy**: There are apps that track your steps, remind you to take your medication, or even help you meditate—all thanks to AI.

The key takeaway here is that AI's job is to make your life more convenient. It's like having a personal assistant that's always ready to help out with everyday tasks.

AI is Here to Help, Not Replace

One concern many people have when they hear about AI is whether it will replace jobs or take over tasks that humans normally do. The truth is, AI isn't here to replace people—it's here to help them. Think of AI as a tool, like a hammer or a calculator. Just as a calculator helps you do math faster but doesn't replace your ability to think, AI helps you with certain tasks without taking away your control.

For example, when your phone suggests a quicker route home or helps you set up a video call, it's not taking over—it's simply offering you helpful suggestions based on what it knows. You are still in charge and can choose whether or not to use its help.

Why Seniors Should Embrace AI

AI is not just for younger generations. In fact, there are many ways it can be particularly useful for seniors. Whether it's helping with daily reminders, simplifying communication with family, or providing entertainment, AI can greatly improve quality of life as we age. For instance:

- **Health Tracking**: AI can help you monitor your health with apps that remind you to take your medication or track your physical activity, making it easier to manage your wellbeing.
- **Staying Social**: AI-powered video calling apps like Zoom or Skype can make it easier to stay connected with family and friends, no matter where they are.
- **Learning New Things**: Want to learn a new language or hobby? AI-powered learning apps like Duolingo can guide you step-by-step.

The best part is that these tools are designed to be simple and easy to use, so you don't need to be tech-savvy to get started.

Hands-On Exercise: Meet Your AI Assistant

Let's try a simple exercise to get comfortable with AI. If you have a smartphone or a tablet with you, try talking to your voice assistant. Here's how:

- **iPhone**: Press and hold the Home button or say "Hey Siri," and then ask something like, "What's the weather today?"
- **Android**: Say "Hey Google" or press and hold the Home button, then ask, "What's the news today?"
- **Amazon Alexa**: If you have an Alexa device, say "Alexa, what time is it?"

These assistants are great examples of how AI can answer questions, help with tasks, or even just chat with you. Try asking them a few different questions or giving them commands, like setting a reminder or telling you a joke. The more you interact, the more natural it will feel!

Wrapping Up: The AI Journey Ahead

As we continue through this book, you'll learn more about how AI works, where it's used, and how you can apply it to make your life easier and more enjoyable. Don't worry if it seems a little overwhelming at first. Just remember that AI is here to help, not complicate things.

In the next chapter, we'll dive deeper into what AI actually is and explore how it compares to human intelligence. By the end of this journey, you'll feel confident using AI to simplify and enhance your everyday life.

Key Takeaway: AI is already part of your daily routine, helping you do things faster and more easily. It's a tool designed to assist you, not replace you, and with just a little practice, you can use it to make your life simpler and more convenient.

Next Steps:

- Try using a voice assistant for small tasks like setting a reminder.
- Think about where else you see AI in your daily life (e.g., shopping, email, photos).
- Get ready for the next chapter where we'll explore how AI compares to human intelligence!

Chapter 2: What is Artificial Intelligence?

In our first chapter, we briefly touched on how AI already helps you in daily life. But what exactly is AI? How does it work, and why is it such a big deal today? Let's dive a little deeper into the concept of AI, but don't worry—we'll keep things simple and non-technical.

What Exactly is AI?

Artificial Intelligence, or AI, is when machines or computers are able to perform tasks that usually require human intelligence. This includes things like understanding speech, recognizing objects in a photo, solving problems, and even making decisions.

Think of AI as a really smart helper. It can be trained to do things based on data (information) that it has been given. The more information or data it has, the better it becomes at understanding what to do. It's similar to how we learn through experience. The more times we try something, the better we get at it. AI works in much the same way—by learning from lots of examples.

Examples of AI in Simple Terms

Let's break this down with a couple of simple examples:

- **AI in a GPS**: When you use a GPS app like Google Maps, AI is working in the background. It looks at millions of data points—things like traffic patterns, road closures, and other drivers' routes. The AI then uses this data to recommend the best and fastest route for you. If you take a wrong turn, it immediately recalculates, showing you a new path.

- **AI in Streaming Services**: If you watch Netflix or listen to music on Spotify, AI is constantly learning what you like. For instance, if you watch a lot of mystery shows, AI will start suggesting more mystery content. It does this by analyzing your behavior—what you watch, how long you watch it, and what other people who like mystery shows are watching.

How AI "Thinks" (But Not Really Like a Human)

AI doesn't think or feel like a human. It doesn't have emotions, opinions, or a personal agenda. Instead, AI processes information quickly to make decisions or offer solutions based on patterns and data. In simple terms, it's a really fast problem-solver. If it has enough information about a situation, it can make a recommendation or take action that seems almost human-like.

However, AI isn't perfect. It doesn't always get things right, especially when it encounters something new that it hasn't learned about before. That's why sometimes your AI assistant (like Siri or Alexa) might misunderstand your command or give you a response that doesn't make sense.

Understanding AI Learning: Machine Learning

One of the key things that make AI smart is something called **machine learning**. Don't let the term scare you—it's simpler than it sounds. Machine learning is how AI improves over time. It's a process where an AI system learns from examples, or "training data," and gets better at making decisions.

Here's a basic example: Imagine teaching a young child to recognize dogs. You'd show them pictures of different types of dogs. After seeing enough examples, the child learns what a dog looks like and can identify one even if they see a new breed for the first time.

AI works similarly. If you show it enough pictures of dogs, it will eventually learn to recognize a dog on its own, even if it hasn't seen that specific breed before. This ability to "learn" from experience is what makes machine learning a powerful tool in AI.

The Different Types of AI

There are different levels or types of AI. Let's cover two main categories in a simplified way:

1. **Narrow AI**: This is the type of AI you see and use today. It's good at one specific task. For example, Siri is great at answering questions and setting reminders, but it can't bake you a cake or clean your house. Google Maps is amazing at giving directions, but it can't help you with medical advice. Narrow AI focuses on doing one thing really well.

2. **General AI**: This is the type of AI we see in science fiction movies. It's a system that could do anything a human can do—think, reason, and act across all types of tasks. General AI doesn't exist yet, but researchers are working on it. The AI we use today is still far from this level, so don't worry—robots won't be taking over the world any time soon!

How AI is Different from Simple Computer Programs

Now, you might be wondering: What makes AI different from regular computer programs we've had for years? It all comes down to **learning and adapting**.

A traditional computer program can only do what it's been told to do. For example, a calculator app can do math problems, but it can't learn from those calculations to become better or faster at solving equations. AI, on the other hand, can **learn from experience**. Once it's been trained with enough data, it can start making decisions on its own. For example, after listening to you for a while, Siri or Google Assistant can get better at understanding your voice and your preferences.

AI in the World Around Us

AI isn't just limited to smartphones and computers. It's being used in a wide variety of fields to improve the way we live and work. Here are just a few examples:

- **Healthcare**: AI is helping doctors detect diseases earlier by analyzing medical images and patient data. It can also remind patients to take their medication or track their health conditions.

- **Transportation**: Self-driving cars are powered by AI. These cars use AI to "see" the road, avoid obstacles, and make safe driving decisions.
- **Retail**: When you shop online, AI helps websites recommend products based on your browsing history and previous purchases. This makes your shopping experience faster and more personalized.

AI is all around us, working behind the scenes to make everyday tasks more efficient and personalized. As AI continues to evolve, it will touch even more aspects of life.

Why You Don't Need to Fear AI

There's a lot of talk in the media about how AI might be dangerous or take over jobs. It's natural to feel uncertain about new technology, but AI is primarily a tool—a powerful one, yes, but still just a tool designed to help, not harm. Like any tool, it's up to us to use it responsibly.

For seniors, AI presents a great opportunity. It can make tasks simpler, help you stay connected with loved ones, and even assist with your health. Whether it's setting reminders, helping you find information, or suggesting new shows to watch, AI can be an empowering tool, not something to fear.

Hands-On Exercise: Try Out a New AI-Powered Tool

Now that you understand a bit more about AI, it's time to try something new! Let's explore an AI-powered app or feature on your phone or computer. Here's a simple exercise:

1. **Explore Recommendations**: Open your favorite app—whether it's Netflix, YouTube, or Amazon. Scroll through the recommendations and think about how AI is working to suggest things you might like. Try clicking on a few recommendations to see how close they match your interests.

2. **Ask for Help**: Use your voice assistant (like Siri or Google Assistant) and ask it to perform a new task. For example, try asking, "What's a good recipe for tonight's dinner?" or "Find a fun game for seniors."

The more you interact with AI, the better it will get at understanding your preferences and helping you in ways that feel personalized.

Wrapping Up: AI is a Helper, Not a Replacement

To summarize, AI is all about machines and computers performing tasks that usually require human intelligence. Whether it's through machine learning or simply analyzing data, AI can assist with everything from finding directions to suggesting new shows. And while AI might sound complicated, it's designed to make life easier for all of us—especially seniors who want tools to simplify everyday tasks.

In the next chapter, we'll dive into the difference between AI and robots, and clear up some common misconceptions. You'll be surprised to learn that most AI doesn't involve physical robots at all!

Key Takeaway: AI is a powerful tool that helps machines learn and improve over time. It's not something to fear but something to embrace, especially as it becomes more useful in our daily lives.

Next Steps:

- Try using an AI-powered app like Netflix or Amazon and explore its recommendations.
- Ask your voice assistant to perform a new task.
- Think about other areas of your life where AI might already be helping without you even realizing it.

Chapter 3: AI vs. Robots: What's the Difference?

When most people hear the word "AI," they think of robots—like the ones in sci-fi movies that walk, talk, and do all sorts of amazing things. But here's the thing: AI and robots are not the same. They often get confused, but they serve different purposes.

What is a Robot?

A robot is a **physical machine** designed to perform tasks. Robots can be as simple as a vacuum cleaner or as complex as a machine that assembles cars. Some robots are controlled by humans, while others can move and act on their own. But by themselves, robots are just machines. They don't "think" or "learn" without some help.

How AI and Robots Work Together

Here's where AI comes in: AI can be the "brain" inside a robot. AI allows a robot to make decisions and learn from experience. Think of a robot like a body, and AI like its brain. Without AI, a robot might only be able to follow very basic instructions. With AI, it can learn how to do things more efficiently or adapt to changes in its environment. For example:

- **Roomba Vacuum**: This small robot can clean your floors. Early versions just followed a random path, bumping into things and changing direction. Newer models use AI to learn your home's layout, avoid obstacles, and clean more efficiently.
- **Self-Driving Cars**: These cars use AI to navigate roads, recognize stop signs, and avoid other vehicles. The AI is constantly "thinking" and adjusting the car's actions based on what it sees and learns.

Why This Matters for You

You don't need a robot to benefit from AI. In fact, most of the AI you use daily doesn't involve physical machines at all. When you talk to your smartphone's voice assistant, send an email, or browse Netflix, you're using AI—no robots required!

Hands-On Exercise: Spot the Difference

Look around your home and see if you can identify any devices that use AI or robots. Does your vacuum use AI? How about your smartphone? Write down a few examples and think about how they help make your life easier.

Chapter 4: Everyday AI: Where You See It Now

AI may sound like something from the future, but it's already all around you, helping in ways you might not even realize. Let's explore some of the most common ways you're already using AI in your daily life.

AI on Your Smartphone

Most modern smartphones are packed with AI features. Here are a few examples:

- **Voice Assistants**: Siri (on iPhones), Google Assistant (on Android phones), and Alexa (on Amazon devices) are all powered by AI. You can ask them to set reminders, play music, or answer questions—AI helps them understand your requests.
- **Camera Enhancements**: When you take a photo, AI adjusts lighting, focuses on faces, and sometimes even suggests filters to make the photo look better.
- **Text Suggestions**: When you're typing a message or email, you might notice your phone suggesting words or completing your sentences. This is AI at work, learning from how you type.

AI in Streaming Services

AI helps you find movies and shows you'll enjoy. When you open Netflix, it doesn't just show random suggestions. It looks at what you've watched before, what others with similar tastes have watched, and recommends new things based on that. Spotify does the same for music.

AI in Shopping

Ever notice how Amazon or other shopping websites suggest items you might like? That's AI analyzing your previous searches and purchases to recommend products. It's like having a personal shopping assistant.

AI in Healthcare

AI is becoming a big part of healthcare. From apps that track your steps and heart rate to tools that help doctors diagnose diseases, AI is making healthcare more personalized and accurate. Some apps can even remind you to take your medication or suggest simple exercises based on your health data.

Hands-On Exercise: Explore AI in Your Apps

Pick two apps you use frequently (like a streaming service or health app). Spend a few minutes exploring how they use AI. Notice any suggestions or adjustments the apps make for you? Write down how AI helps you in each app.

Chapter 5: How AI Learns: The Concept of Machine Learning

At this point, you know that AI can learn from data and get better over time. But how does this actually work? Let's break it down in simple terms with the idea of **machine learning**.

What is Machine Learning?

Machine learning is when AI is trained to recognize patterns and make decisions based on examples. It's similar to how humans learn from experience. For example, if you've been baking cookies for years, you know the dough should feel a certain way. The more you bake, the better you get at it. Machine learning works in a similar way, but instead of learning from hands-on practice, AI learns from **data**.

An Easy Example: Email Spam Filters

Have you noticed that most spam emails (junk mail) never make it to your inbox? That's because AI is using machine learning to spot them. Over time, email services like Gmail learn what spam looks like by analyzing the words, links, and patterns in millions of emails. Once the AI system has seen enough examples of spam, it learns to block them automatically.

AI and Photos

Another example is when your phone recognizes faces in photos. The AI has been shown thousands (even millions) of faces during its "training." Once it's learned enough, it can recognize a face in any new photo you take.

How AI Keeps Getting Better

One of the amazing things about machine learning is that the more data AI gets, the smarter it becomes. For instance, the more you use your voice assistant (like Siri or Alexa), the better it gets at understanding your voice and preferences. It's constantly learning and improving based on how you interact with it.

Hands-On Exercise: Voice Assistant Training
If you use a voice assistant (Siri, Google Assistant, or Alexa), try giving it a few new commands today. Over time, the AI will get better at understanding your voice, even if you speak in different tones or accents. Try asking it a question you've never asked before, and see how it responds.

Chapter 6: Demystifying Algorithms

You've probably heard the word **algorithm** before. It might sound complicated, but at its core, an algorithm is just a set of rules a computer follows to solve a problem or make a decision. In the world of AI, algorithms are what make everything work behind the scenes.

What is an Algorithm?

Think of an algorithm like a recipe. When you follow a recipe to bake a cake, you're using a set of steps in a certain order to get the result you want (a delicious cake!). Similarly, an algorithm is a set of steps the AI follows to complete a task.

For example:

- **Search Engines**: When you type something into Google, an algorithm determines which websites to show you based on what's most relevant to your search.
- **Online Shopping**: When Amazon recommends products, an algorithm is sorting through thousands of possibilities to find the ones it thinks you'll like best.

Algorithms and AI

When AI uses machine learning, it relies on algorithms to analyze data and learn from it. Algorithms help AI figure out patterns, make decisions, and adjust to new situations. For instance, the algorithm behind a voice assistant helps it understand the words you say and find the best response.

Algorithms in Everyday Life

You encounter algorithms more often than you might think:

- **Weather Apps**: These apps use algorithms to predict the weather based on data from past weather patterns.
- **Social Media**: Have you noticed how your Facebook or

Instagram feed shows posts from people you interact with the most? That's because an algorithm is deciding what content you're most likely to enjoy.

Hands-On Exercise: Track an Algorithm in Action

The next time you use a search engine (like Google) or an app that recommends something (like YouTube or Netflix), take a moment to think about the algorithm behind it. What kind of recommendations are you seeing? Why do you think those results came up first? Write down how you think the algorithm helped you find what you needed.

Chapter 7: The Evolution of AI: From Past to Present

AI might seem like a modern invention, but the idea of creating intelligent machines has been around for centuries. Let's take a brief journey through the history of AI, from early dreams of mechanical minds to the powerful AI we have today.

Early Ideas of Artificial Intelligence

The idea of creating machines that can think has fascinated humans for a long time. Ancient myths from Greece and China spoke of mechanical men, and in the 19th century, inventors started creating simple machines that could perform specific tasks.

One early example is the **automaton**—a mechanical figure that could mimic human actions, like playing chess or writing. These machines were impressive but far from intelligent. They didn't "think" or learn; they were just cleverly built to follow pre-set movements.

The Birth of Modern AI

The real breakthrough came in the 1950s when scientists began wondering: What if we could create a machine that can learn and solve problems like a human? The term **Artificial Intelligence** was first used in 1956, and researchers began developing programs that could play games, solve math problems, and even learn simple tasks.

In the following decades, AI research expanded. Computers became more powerful, and AI started to solve more complex problems. For example, in 1997, an AI program called **Deep Blue** beat the world champion at chess—a milestone that showed AI could compete with human intelligence in specific tasks.

AI Today: In Your Pocket and Home

Fast forward to today, and AI is no longer just for researchers or scientists. It's in your smartphone, your TV, and even your home appliances. Thanks to **machine learning**, AI systems can learn from huge amounts of data and get better over time.

AI is helping doctors detect diseases, powering virtual assistants like Alexa, and even helping self-driving cars navigate. And the best part is, you don't need to be an expert to use it—AI is designed to be user-friendly and accessible to everyone, including seniors.

Hands-On Exercise: Learn About AI's Past

Do a quick online search for the term "Deep Blue vs. Garry Kasparov" and read a bit about how an AI beat a world chess champion. Write down how you feel about AI's progress from the 1950s to now. Does it surprise you?

Chapter 8: AI in Your Phone: Smart Assistants

One of the most helpful and easiest ways to use AI is through **smart assistants** like Siri, Google Assistant, and Alexa. These voice-activated tools can help you with everyday tasks, answer questions, and even control smart devices in your home—all without you needing to lift a finger.

What Can Smart Assistants Do?

Smart assistants can do a lot! Here are some ways they can help you:

- **Set reminders**: "Hey Siri, remind me to take my medication at 9 a.m."
- **Check the weather**: "Alexa, what's the weather tomorrow?"
- **Play music**: "Hey Google, play some relaxing music."
- **Get answers**: "Hey Siri, how many cups are in a quart?"
- **Control smart devices**: If you have smart lights, thermostats, or plugs, you can control them by saying, "Alexa, turn off the lights."

These assistants use **natural language processing (NLP)**, a form of AI that allows them to understand spoken language. This means they can respond to your voice commands just like a real assistant would!

How Smart Assistants Learn

The more you use your smart assistant, the better it gets at understanding your preferences. Over time, it will learn your routines—like when you usually wake up, what kind of music you enjoy, or how often you ask for reminders. This is AI at work, constantly learning and improving to serve you better.

Why It's Useful for Seniors

For seniors, smart assistants can be a game-changer. They make tasks easier and more accessible, especially for those who may have difficulty typing or navigating apps. Whether you need help setting reminders for medications, finding recipes, or staying connected with loved ones, a smart assistant can do the job quickly and hands-free.

Hands-On Exercise: Set Up Your First Command

If you haven't used a smart assistant before, try giving it a command today. For example, say, "Hey Google, remind me to call my daughter tomorrow at 10 a.m." or "Hey Siri, play classical music." It's simple and fun!

Chapter 9: Voice Commands: Making AI Work for You

Using AI isn't just about asking questions; it's also about giving **commands** to make everyday life easier. With voice commands, you can operate many devices hands-free. Let's explore how voice commands can simplify your daily tasks.

How Voice Commands Work

When you give a voice command, AI breaks down your speech into **keywords** and **actions**. For example, if you say, "Alexa, turn off the lights," the AI identifies that you want to perform an action ("turn off") and applies it to the right object (the "lights").

Everyday Tasks You Can Control with Your Voice

Here are some simple voice commands you can try at home:

- **Make a phone call**: "Hey Siri, call John."
- **Send a text message**: "Hey Google, send a text to Karen saying 'I'll be there soon.'"
- **Set alarms and timers**: "Alexa, set a timer for 10 minutes."
- **Check appointments**: "Hey Google, what's on my calendar today?"
- **Control smart devices**: If you have smart plugs or lights, you can say, "Alexa, turn on the fan," or "Hey Google, dim the lights to 50%."

Benefits for Seniors

For seniors, using voice commands can reduce the need for typing, tapping, or navigating through apps. Whether you have mobility issues or simply want a faster way to get things done, voice commands can make daily tasks smoother and more convenient.

Hands-On Exercise: Use a Voice Command to Control a Device

If you have a smart speaker or smart device at home, try using voice commands to control it. For example, say, "Alexa, turn off the living room lights" or "Hey Google, turn on the coffee maker." See how easy it is to control your home with just your voice!

Chapter 10: AI in Smart Devices: TVs, Thermostats, and More

Smart assistants aren't the only AI-powered devices that can improve your life. Many everyday appliances and devices are becoming "smart," meaning they use AI to adapt to your preferences and make tasks easier. Let's explore some of the most useful smart devices and how they work.

What is a Smart Device?

A smart device is any appliance or gadget that connects to the internet and can be controlled remotely or by voice commands. These devices often use AI to learn your habits and adjust their settings accordingly. Some examples include:

- **Smart TVs**: These TVs can recommend shows based on what you watch and allow you to control them with your voice.
- **Smart Thermostats**: These devices learn your heating and cooling preferences and adjust the temperature automatically to save energy.
- **Smart Lights**: You can control these lights with your voice or an app, adjusting brightness and color to match your mood.
- **Smart Plugs**: These plugs allow you to turn any regular appliance (like a coffee maker or lamp) into a smart device that you can control remotely.

How Smart Devices Learn

Smart devices often use **machine learning** to understand your preferences over time. For example, a smart thermostat might notice that you like your home warmer in the mornings and cooler in the evenings. Over time, it will automatically adjust the temperature to fit your routine, without you needing to do anything.

Chapter 11: Navigating with AI: Google Maps and GPS

One of the most practical uses of AI is navigation. Whether you're driving, walking, or taking public transportation, AI-powered tools like **Google Maps** help you find the best route, avoid traffic, and even suggest nearby places to visit. Let's take a deeper dive into how AI improves navigation and makes travel easier for everyone, including seniors.

How Does AI Power Navigation?

Google Maps and other GPS apps use AI to analyze **real-time data** from millions of users. This data includes traffic conditions, user locations, and route options. AI processes this information almost instantly to provide you with the best route, as well as updates on any changes that could affect your trip. Here's a breakdown of how AI helps you navigate:

- **Traffic Conditions**: AI looks at current traffic, road closures, accidents, and even weather conditions. For example, if there's an unexpected accident on your usual route, AI will detect it and suggest an alternate route to avoid delays.

- **User Locations**: AI doesn't just rely on one person's data. It uses data from millions of other drivers and walkers to estimate how long your trip will take. By learning from the experiences of others, AI can help you find the quickest or easiest route.

- **Route Options**: AI analyzes different paths you could take to your destination, comparing them based on factors like distance, time, and current road conditions. It often provides several options, allowing you to choose the one that works best for you, whether you want to avoid highways, tolls, or traffic jams.

Turn-by-Turn Directions: AI as Your Travel Companion

One of the best features of AI-powered navigation is its **turn-by-turn directions**. This means the app will guide you every step of the way, telling you when and where to turn, and even rerouting you if something changes mid-trip. This is especially useful in unfamiliar areas or if you're unsure about road conditions.

For instance, if you're driving to a new location, Google Maps will give clear instructions like, "In 500 feet, turn left onto Main Street." But AI goes beyond simple directions—it's constantly updating based on real-time data. If there's a traffic jam ahead, it may suggest a detour. If you miss a turn, it will quickly recalculate the route and get you back on track.

Example: Rerouting in Real Time

Imagine you're driving to a doctor's appointment. Halfway there, you hit unexpected roadwork. Without AI, you might be stuck waiting in traffic or forced to pull over and figure out an alternate route on your own. But with AI, your GPS will immediately detect the roadwork and suggest a faster way around it, possibly saving you time and stress.

AI-Powered Walking Directions: Getting Around with Ease

AI isn't just for drivers. It's also great for **walking directions**. Whether you're taking a casual walk in your neighborhood, exploring a new park, or navigating through a large building like a shopping mall or hospital, AI can guide you with clear, step-by-step instructions.

Google Maps, for example, can tell you the best walking routes, suggest **scenic paths**, and even show you sidewalks and crosswalks for safer navigation. It can also estimate how long your walk will take and provide updates if there are any obstacles like construction along the way.

Example: Exploring a New City

Let's say you're visiting a new city and want to take a stroll through a historic district. Instead of worrying about where to go or getting lost, you can use Google Maps' walking directions. AI will guide you along streets and point out landmarks, restaurants, or attractions nearby. This makes exploring stress-free and more enjoyable.

AI and Public Transportation: A Time-Saving Tool

For those who rely on **public transportation**, AI makes using buses, trains, and subways much simpler. Google Maps offers real-time updates on schedules, delays, and routes, ensuring that you get where you need to go efficiently. With AI, you can:

- See **arrival times** for the next bus or train in real-time.
- Get notifications about **delays or service changes**.
- Find the quickest way to get from point A to point B, including connections between different forms of transport (like taking a bus to a train station).

Example: Navigating a Train Station

Imagine you're at a busy train station and need to find your platform quickly. Instead of feeling overwhelmed, you can open Google Maps, which will tell you exactly which train to catch, where it's located, and how long until it arrives. It even shows platform numbers and updates in case of delays.

Why AI Navigation is Useful for Seniors

For seniors, AI-powered navigation can be a life-changing tool. Not only does it provide clear, easy-to-follow directions, but it also eliminates the stress of getting lost or dealing with unexpected traffic. With AI helping you plan your routes, you can feel more confident and independent, whether you're driving to a doctor's appointment, walking through your neighborhood, or catching a bus to meet a friend.

Safety and convenience are key. AI ensures that you're always updated on current road or traffic conditions, allowing you to adjust your plans without hassle. Plus, AI's voice-guided instructions mean you don't need to keep looking at a map—just listen and follow the directions.

Hands-On Exercise: Plan and Test a Route Using Google Maps

1. **Step 1: Open Google Maps**

   On your smartphone or computer, open Google Maps. If you haven't used it before, download the app from your device's app store (it's free).

2. **Step 2: Enter Your Destination**

   Enter a location you're planning to visit, such as a nearby park, grocery store, or relative's house. Google Maps will instantly suggest the best routes for walking, driving, or public transport.

3. **Step 3: Explore Your Route Options**

   Take a moment to explore the different routes AI suggests. Compare the fastest, scenic, or toll-free routes. Click on each option to see how long it will take and what traffic conditions might be like.

4. **Step 4: Turn on Voice Guidance**

   If you're driving or walking, turn on **voice-guided navigation** so you don't need to look at the screen while you're on the move. Try following its directions for a short trip and notice how AI adjusts to any changes or missed turns.

5. **Bonus Step: Explore Landmarks**

   If you're in a new area, use the "Explore" function on Google Maps to find landmarks, cafes, or attractions nearby. AI will suggest popular places based on your location and interests.

Chapter 12: AI in Entertainment: Music, Movies, and TV (

AI doesn't just help with navigation—it also makes it easier to discover new **music, movies, and TV shows**. AI-powered recommendation systems help you find entertainment tailored to your tastes, saving you the trouble of scrolling through endless options.

How AI Recommends Content

When you watch a show on Netflix or listen to a playlist on Spotify, AI learns about your preferences. It notices the genres you like, the time of day you watch or listen, and how often you revisit certain types of content. Using this data, AI can suggest movies, shows, or songs that align with your tastes.

Here's how AI works behind the scenes on popular platforms:

- **Netflix**: Netflix's AI looks at your viewing history and compares it to the habits of other users with similar preferences. If you've been watching comedies, Netflix will suggest more comedies that people like you have enjoyed. It even considers factors like the time of day, recommending lighter shows in the morning and more dramatic ones in the evening.

- **Spotify**: AI creates playlists like "Discover Weekly" or "Release Radar" based on your listening habits. It groups together songs and artists similar to those you've enjoyed before, introducing you to new music without you needing to search for it.

- **YouTube**: YouTube's recommendation engine suggests videos based on your watch history, likes, and even how long you've watched certain types of content. If you've been watching cooking tutorials, it might recommend more cooking-related videos or channels.

Benefits of AI Recommendations for Seniors

For seniors, AI makes finding entertainment much simpler. Instead of browsing through hundreds of movies or songs, AI narrows down your choices to what you're most likely to enjoy. This can save time and reduce frustration, especially if you're not sure what you're in the mood for.

Example: Personalized Movie Suggestions on Netflix

If you've been watching British mysteries or family dramas, Netflix will highlight new shows and movies from those genres. You'll also see popular recommendations based on what's trending among other viewers with similar tastes. This means more time watching and less time searching!

Voice-Controlled Entertainment with AI

Many smart TVs and streaming devices allow you to use **voice commands** to find and play content. For example, if you have a smart TV or use a streaming device like a Fire Stick, you can simply say, "Alexa, play a comedy," and AI will pull up a selection of comedies for you.

This is especially helpful if you find it difficult to navigate menus or type with a remote. By using your voice, you can easily browse through Netflix, YouTube, or Amazon Prime Video without having to lift a finger.

Example: Using Voice Commands to Play Music

Imagine you want to listen to a relaxing playlist while cooking dinner. Instead of scrolling through your music app, you can say, "Hey Siri, play relaxing jazz," and AI will select a playlist based on your preferences. If you've used this command before, AI will even remember which playlist you liked and play it automatically.

AI-Enhanced Playlists and Auto-Play

One of the most useful features of AI in entertainment is its ability to create customized playlists. On Spotify, you may have seen "Discover Weekly," a playlist of songs AI thinks you'll like based on your previous listening habits. Similarly, Netflix's "Continue Watching" and "Recommended For You" sections are powered by AI, which helps you pick up where you left off or find something new.

- **Auto-Play**: You may have noticed that after you finish watching a show or video, the platform immediately starts playing something similar. This is AI's way of ensuring you stay engaged, providing content related to what you just watched.

Example: Discovering New Music on Spotify

If you listen to a lot of jazz, Spotify's AI will add new jazz artists and songs to your "Discover Weekly" playlist. Over time, it will refine its suggestions, introducing you to artists you may not have found on your own.

Hands-On Exercise: Explore AI's Entertainment Recommendations

1. **Step 1: Open Your Streaming App**
   Open Netflix, Spotify, or YouTube on your device. Take a moment to notice the recommendations AI has generated for you.
2. **Step 2: Choose a Recommendation**
   Pick one movie, song, or video from the list of AI-suggested content. Watch or listen to it, and then reflect on whether it matched your tastes.
3. **Step 3: Try Voice Commands**
   If you have a smart speaker or voice-controlled remote, try using voice commands. For example, say, "Alexa, play my favorite playlist," or "Hey Google, show me a comedy movie."
4. **Bonus Step: Create a Playlist**

On Spotify or a similar music platform, let AI create a playlist for you. Explore the "Discover Weekly" or "Made For You" playlists and see what new artists or songs it introduces to you.

34

Chapter 13: AI and Your Health: Fitness Trackers and Health Apps

AI is playing an increasingly important role in helping people, especially seniors, maintain and improve their health. Whether through fitness trackers, health apps, or even AI-powered reminders, this technology can assist in staying active, managing medication, and tracking your well-being.

AI in Fitness Trackers

You might have heard of popular fitness trackers like **Fitbit**, **Apple Watch**, or even basic pedometers. These devices use AI to monitor your physical activity and provide insights into your health. They collect data like the number of steps you've taken, your heart rate, calories burned, and even your sleep patterns. AI then processes this data and offers personalized suggestions to help you stay on track with your fitness goals.

For example:

- **Step Count and Activity Goals**: Many fitness trackers encourage you to reach a daily step goal, such as 5,000 or 10,000 steps. AI tracks your movement throughout the day and reminds you to stay active if you haven't hit your target.
- **Heart Rate Monitoring**: AI-powered devices like the Apple Watch monitor your heart rate continuously and notify you if something seems off, like an unusually high or low pulse.
- **Sleep Tracking**: AI can track your sleep patterns, telling you how long you slept and the quality of that sleep. If you're tossing and turning, AI might suggest ways to improve your rest, such as going to bed earlier or adjusting your sleeping environment.

How AI Uses Your Health Data

The power of AI lies in its ability to **learn from your behavior**. Over time, AI becomes more accurate at understanding your health patterns. For example, if you always take a walk after lunch, AI will start recognizing this habit and might even suggest longer routes to improve your fitness. Similarly, if you haven't been active for a few days, AI might encourage you to get moving again with gentle reminders.

Example: Personalized Exercise Suggestions

Imagine you wear a Fitbit, and it notices that you're regularly meeting your step goal but not doing enough aerobic exercise (activities that increase your heart rate). The AI might suggest you try a brisk walk or light jogging, sending a reminder at a time you usually go for a stroll. This helps keep your fitness routine varied and effective.

AI in Health Apps: Tracking Medication and Doctor Visits

Beyond fitness, AI is making it easier to stay on top of your overall health. Health apps powered by AI can track your **medication schedule**, remind you of upcoming doctor's appointments, and even suggest lifestyle changes based on your health data.

For example:

- **Medication Reminders**: Apps like **MediSafe** use AI to remind you when to take your medications. If you skip a dose, the app will send a notification and help you track your medication intake over time.
- **Symptom Checkers**: Some health apps, like **Ada Health** or **WebMD**, use AI to help you identify potential causes of symptoms. You input your symptoms, and AI suggests possible conditions or whether you should seek medical attention.
- **Exercise and Diet Suggestions**: If you're trying to lose weight or manage a condition like diabetes, AI-powered apps like **MyFitnessPal** can recommend meal plans or workout

routines based on your goals and health status.

Why AI is Useful for Senior Health

For seniors, staying on top of health concerns can be overwhelming, especially if you take multiple medications or manage chronic conditions. AI helps by simplifying these tasks and acting as a virtual assistant, offering reminders, tracking progress, and making personalized recommendations to keep you on track.

Hands-On Exercise: Explore AI-Health Tools

1. **Step 1: Try a Fitness Tracker**
   If you have a fitness tracker or health app on your phone, start by wearing the device or opening the app. Track your steps or monitor your heart rate for a few days to get a sense of how AI provides feedback on your activity.

2. **Step 2: Set a Goal**
   Set a daily activity goal—like walking 5,000 steps—and let AI remind you to stay active. Notice how it adapts to your habits and progress.

3. **Step 3: Explore a Health App**
   Download a health app like MediSafe or MyFitnessPal and enter some basic health information. Explore how AI helps with medication reminders or exercise plans, and try setting up a few notifications to help you stay on top of your health routine.

Chapter 14: Online Shopping and AI Recommendations

AI is transforming how we shop online, making it easier, faster, and more personalized. Whether you're shopping on **Amazon**, browsing for gifts, or just looking for the best deals, AI helps by suggesting products based on your preferences and shopping habits. In this chapter, we'll explore how AI simplifies online shopping and ensures you get the best products for your needs.

How AI Powers Online Shopping

When you shop online, AI is constantly working in the background to make your experience smoother. Have you ever noticed how **Amazon** or **eBay** recommends products to you as soon as you log in? That's AI analyzing your previous purchases, searches, and browsing history to predict what you might be interested in.

Here's how AI helps with your online shopping experience:

- **Product Recommendations**: AI suggests items based on what you've bought before. For example, if you often buy gardening tools, the next time you log in, AI might show you related products like seeds or watering cans.

- **Price Comparisons**: AI can help you find the best deals by comparing prices across different sellers. Some shopping apps, like **Honey** or **PriceGrabber**, use AI to track price changes and alert you when an item you're interested in is on sale.

- **Personalized Coupons**: Retailers often send personalized coupons based on your shopping habits. If AI detects that you frequently buy a certain type of product, like vitamins or home supplies, it might offer you a discount the next time you visit the site.

AI and Smart Shopping Assistants

Many shopping platforms now offer **smart assistants** that help you find products and make purchases with just a few voice commands. For example, **Alexa** on Amazon allows you to say, "Alexa, add toothpaste to my shopping list," and the AI will automatically place the item in your online cart.

These assistants are perfect for when you're multitasking or just want to avoid the hassle of navigating through websites. You can even ask them to check the status of an order or reorder an item you've purchased before.

Example: Smart Shopping with Alexa

Imagine you're running low on coffee. Instead of going to your computer or phone, you can simply say, "Alexa, reorder my coffee," and AI will find the brand and type you've ordered previously, adding it to your cart for easy checkout.

AI in Grocery Shopping

AI is also becoming popular in **grocery shopping**. Many apps now let you create grocery lists based on your past purchases. For example, **Walmart** and **Instacart** use AI to suggest groceries you might need based on what you've bought before. Some AI-powered apps can even **suggest recipes** and automatically generate a shopping list for you.

Example: Automatic Grocery Lists

If you frequently buy bread, milk, and eggs, AI will recognize this pattern. The next time you log into the app, it will pre-fill your cart with these items, making your shopping quicker and easier.

Why AI Shopping is Helpful for Seniors

For seniors, online shopping can be a convenient and time-saving way to get everything you need without leaving the house. AI improves the shopping experience by helping you discover new products, find discounts, and automate tasks like reordering essentials.

AI also ensures that you don't forget important purchases. If you regularly buy vitamins or household goods, AI will remind you when you're running low, ensuring that you're always stocked up on the items you need.

Hands-On Exercise: Try AI for Online Shopping

1. **Step 1: Log into an Online Store**
   Open your favorite online shopping website, like Amazon or Walmart. Take a moment to notice the product recommendations on the homepage. How many of them match items you've purchased before?

2. **Step 2: Use a Shopping Assistant**
   If you have a smart speaker like Alexa or Google Home, try adding an item to your shopping list with your voice. For example, say, "Alexa, add shampoo to my shopping list," and see how AI handles your request.

3. **Step 3: Explore Discounts with AI**
   Download a price comparison app like Honey or CamelCamelCamel. Search for a product you're interested in and let AI show you if the price has dropped or if there are discounts available.

Chapter 15: AI for Seniors: Virtual Companions and Assistive Technologies

AI is revolutionizing assistive technologies, offering new ways for seniors to stay connected, safe, and supported. From **virtual companions** that can chat with you to **assistive devices** that help with daily tasks, AI is making it easier to maintain independence and enhance well-being.

Virtual Companions: AI for Conversation and Socialization

One of the most innovative uses of AI is in **virtual companions**—programs designed to have conversations, provide emotional support, and even remind you of important tasks. Virtual companions are ideal for seniors who may feel isolated or want someone to chat with regularly.

For example, AI-powered companions like **Elliq** or **Replika** can:

- **Engage in conversations**: These virtual companions can ask about your day, share the news, or even play games with you. They use **natural language processing** to understand and respond to your questions or comments, making conversations feel natural.

- **Remind you of tasks**: Elliq, for example, can remind you to take medication, drink water, or stay active throughout the day. It's like having a friendly, tech-savvy companion who looks out for your well-being.

- **Provide emotional support**: Virtual companions are designed to offer companionship, helping seniors who might feel lonely. While they can't replace human connections, they can offer regular interaction, especially when family members or friends aren't available to chat.

Example: A Chat with Elliq

Imagine waking up and saying, "Elliq, what's the weather today?" The companion responds with today's forecast, then asks how you slept and if you need any reminders for the day. It's a gentle, friendly interaction that helps you start your morning with a little company.

Assistive Devices: AI Helping with Daily Tasks

AI is also improving traditional **assistive devices**. From smart hearing aids to devices that remind you to take your medication, AI can provide personalized support tailored to your needs.

- **Smart Hearing Aids**: Devices like **Oticon** or **Widex** use AI to adjust sound levels based on your environment. If you're in a noisy room, the hearing aid will automatically lower background noise and focus on the person speaking to you.

- **AI-Powered Medication Dispensers**: Devices like **Hero** use AI to manage medication schedules. You simply fill the machine with your medications, and it dispenses the right dose at the right time, sending alerts to your phone if you forget.

- **Fall Detection and Emergency Alerts**: AI-powered devices like **Life Alert** or smartwatches with fall detection can automatically contact emergency services if they detect a fall or health issue, ensuring help is on the way even if you can't reach a phone.

Why AI Assistive Technologies Matter for Seniors

These technologies offer a **sense of security** and independence, allowing seniors to age in place safely. Virtual companions provide social interaction, while assistive devices ensure important tasks—like taking medication or staying safe—are managed with the help of AI.

For seniors who live alone, AI can act as a second set of eyes and ears, making sure you're supported even when caregivers aren't around. This can improve quality of life and offer peace of mind for both seniors and their families.

Hands-On Exercise: Try a Virtual Companion

1. **Step 1: Download or Explore a Virtual Companion**
   If you're interested in chatting with a virtual companion, try downloading an app like **Replika** or explore devices like **Elliq**. Set up a simple conversation by asking basic questions like, "How are you?" or "What's the news today?"

2. **Step 2: Try an Assistive Technology**
   If you use a smart hearing aid or fall detection device, spend some time exploring how the AI works. Check its settings and adjust them to your preferences. If you're curious, look into AI-powered medication reminders or dispensers and see how they can help you stay on top of your health.

Chapter 16: Chatbots: Talking to AI Online

Have you ever visited a website and seen a little box pop up asking if you need help? That's a **chatbot**—an AI-powered assistant that can answer questions, help with customer service, and even troubleshoot problems. Chatbots are becoming a common way to interact with companies and services online, and they make finding information faster and easier.

What is a Chatbot?

A chatbot is a program that uses **Artificial Intelligence (AI)** to simulate a conversation with you. Instead of speaking to a human, you're talking to a computer program that's been trained to understand and respond to common questions. Chatbots are often found on websites, in apps, and even in messaging platforms like **Facebook Messenger**.

They're programmed to help with:

- **Customer service**: Chatbots can help with things like tracking an order, answering frequently asked questions, or scheduling appointments.
- **Product recommendations**: Some chatbots help you find the right product based on your preferences or needs. For example, a chatbot on a clothing website might ask what styles you like and suggest items you'd enjoy.
- **Technical support**: If you have an issue with your phone or a service, a chatbot can guide you through troubleshooting steps before connecting you with a human representative if needed.

How Do Chatbots Work?

Chatbots use **Natural Language Processing (NLP)**, a type of AI that allows them to understand and respond to human language. When you type a question like, "How do I reset my password?" the chatbot uses its training to recognize the keywords ("reset" and "password") and gives you an appropriate response.

If the chatbot can't answer your question, it often connects you with a human customer service representative, but by that point, you might have already gotten the help you need without waiting on hold or navigating long menus.

Example: Using a Chatbot for Online Shopping

Let's say you're shopping online and you need to know if a certain item is in stock. Instead of searching the whole website, you click on the chatbot. You type, "Do you have this jacket in medium?" The chatbot checks inventory and responds within seconds, saving you time and effort.

Benefits of Chatbots for Seniors

For seniors, chatbots are a helpful way to get answers quickly without having to navigate complex websites or wait on hold for customer service. If you need help tracking an order, finding information, or troubleshooting a problem, chatbots can simplify the process and make the internet more accessible.

Hands-On Exercise: Try Chatting with a Bot

1. **Step 1: Visit a Website with a Chatbot**
    Go to a website like Amazon, your bank, or a utility provider. Look for a small chat icon, usually in the bottom corner of the page.
2. **Step 2: Ask a Question**
    Click the chat icon and ask a simple question like, "How do I check my order status?" or "What are your store hours?"
3. **Step 3: See How the Bot Responds**
    Notice how quickly the chatbot responds and how clear the

answer is. If you have a more complex question, see if the chatbot connects you to a human representative.

Chapter 17: Using AI to Send Messages and Make Calls

One of the best ways AI can simplify your life is by helping you send messages and make calls, especially with voice commands. Whether you're texting a family member, making a phone call, or even sending an email, AI assistants like **Siri**, **Google Assistant**, and **Alexa** make these tasks hands-free and easy.

How AI Helps with Messaging

Using your voice to send messages is one of the easiest ways to stay connected without having to type. With AI, you can send texts, make calls, or even send emails by simply speaking your request. This is especially helpful if you have trouble with small keyboards or prefer to avoid typing altogether.

Here's how it works:

- **Voice-to-Text**: Simply say, "Send a text to John saying, 'I'll be there at 5 PM.'" The AI processes your voice command, converts it into text, and sends the message for you.
- **Reading Messages Aloud**: If you receive a text message, you can ask your AI assistant to read it out loud. For example, say, "Hey Siri, read my last message," and Siri will tell you what the message says.
- **Sending Emails**: You can also compose and send emails by speaking. Say, "Hey Google, send an email to Emma," and then dictate the content. AI will send it off without you needing to type a single word.

Making Calls with AI

In addition to sending messages, AI can also make phone calls for you. Whether you need to call a family member, a doctor's office, or a restaurant to make a reservation, AI makes it as simple as saying, "Hey Siri, call Sarah."

AI assistants can:

- **Dial contacts**: AI will search your contacts and dial the right number when you ask it to.
- **Redial last call**: You can say, "Alexa, redial my last call," and it will call the last number you spoke to.
- **Voice commands on speaker**: You can ask AI to put calls on speakerphone, making it easier to talk without holding the phone.

Why AI Messaging and Calling is Helpful for Seniors

For seniors who may find it difficult to use touchscreens or type on small keyboards, AI provides an easy, hands-free solution. With just a few simple commands, you can stay in touch with loved ones, schedule appointments, or check in with a friend.

Hands-On Exercise: Send a Message with Your Voice

1. **Step 1: Open Your AI Assistant**
   On your smartphone, activate Siri, Google Assistant, or Alexa by saying "Hey Siri" or "Hey Google."
2. **Step 2: Send a Message**
   Say, "Send a text to [contact] saying, 'Looking forward to our lunch tomorrow!'" Let AI convert your words into text and send the message.
3. **Step 3: Make a Call**
   Try making a call using a voice command. Say, "Call [contact]" and let the AI assistant dial for you.

Chapter 18: AI in Email: Organizing Your Inbox

Email can sometimes feel overwhelming, especially when you have a lot of unread messages, spam, and important notifications mixed together. AI can help you **organize your inbox**, making it easier to find the messages that matter and get rid of the ones that don't.

How AI Helps with Email Management

AI-powered email services like **Gmail** and **Outlook** use algorithms to automatically filter and categorize your emails. These tools learn from your behavior—such as which emails you open, which ones you delete, and which ones you reply to—and help sort them accordingly.

Here's what AI can do:

- **Filter Spam**: AI automatically detects spam emails and moves them to a separate folder, so you don't have to deal with them in your main inbox. It's constantly learning from millions of users, so it gets better at identifying unwanted messages.

- **Categorize Emails**: AI can separate your emails into different tabs or folders, such as "Primary," "Social," "Promotions," or "Updates." This helps you focus on important emails while placing newsletters, advertisements, and other less urgent messages out of sight.

- **Smart Replies**: Some email services offer **Smart Replies**—short, suggested responses based on the email you received. For example, if someone asks, "Can you meet at 3 PM?" AI might suggest responses like "Yes, that works" or "Can we do 4 PM instead?"

Why AI Email Tools Matter for Seniors

For seniors who want to keep their inboxes organized but don't want to spend a lot of time sorting through messages, AI can help by filtering out the clutter and highlighting important emails. This makes it easier to focus on what matters and avoid missing key messages.

Hands-On Exercise: Organize Your Inbox with AI

1. **Step 1: Open Your Email**
   Open your email app (Gmail, Outlook, etc.) and take note of how your emails are categorized. Do you see tabs or folders like "Primary" and "Promotions"?

2. **Step 2: Check Your Spam Folder**
   Look inside your spam folder to see if AI has correctly identified unwanted messages. Notice how these messages are filtered automatically.

3. **Step 3: Try Smart Replies**
   If you use Gmail or another service with Smart Replies, try responding to an email using one of the suggested replies. See how AI helps you compose messages quickly.

Chapter 19: Video Calls Made Easy with AI

Staying connected with family and friends through **video calls** has never been easier, thanks to AI. Video calling platforms like **Zoom**, **Skype**, and **Google Meet** use AI to improve the quality of calls and ensure you have a smooth experience, even if you're new to the technology.

How AI Enhances Video Calls

Video calling apps use AI to ensure that your video and audio are clear, even if your internet connection isn't perfect. AI helps with:

- **Noise cancellation**: AI filters out background noise, so if you're in a noisy environment, the person on the other end can still hear you clearly. This is great for blocking out things like barking dogs or TV sounds.

- **Improved video quality**: AI automatically adjusts your video settings, ensuring you look clear even if the lighting in your room isn't ideal. It can brighten dark spaces or reduce glare from bright lights.

- **Automatic captions**: Some platforms, like Google Meet, offer **live captions**, where AI transcribes what's being said in real-time. This can be especially useful if you have hearing difficulties.

How to Set Up a Video Call with AI Help

Setting up a video call with AI assistance is straightforward, and most platforms guide you through the process with easy-to-follow steps.

- **Zoom**: Simply download the app, sign up for an account, and click "New Meeting" to start a call. Zoom's AI adjusts video quality based on your internet connection and can mute background noise automatically.

- **Google Meet**: You can start a video call directly from Gmail or your Google Calendar. Google Meet offers AI-generated live captions during the call.
- **Skype**: Once you've downloaded the Skype app, you can search for contacts and start a video call with a single click. Skype's AI optimizes video and sound quality during your call.

Why Video Calls with AI Are Useful for Seniors

Video calls allow seniors to stay in touch with loved ones, even if they're far away. With AI improving sound and video quality, you don't need to worry about technical issues getting in the way of a good conversation. Plus, the simplicity of AI-guided setups means you can get connected quickly.

Hands-On Exercise: Set Up a Video Call

1. **Step 1: Choose a Platform**
   Pick a video call platform like Zoom, Skype, or Google Meet. Download the app if you don't have it yet.

2. **Step 2: Start a Test Call**
   Start a test call with a family member or friend. Explore how AI improves video and audio quality.

3. **Step 3: Turn on Captions**
   If you're using Google Meet, try enabling live captions to see how AI can transcribe speech during the call.

Chapter 20: Speech Recognition: Talking, Typing, and Transcribing

One of the most useful AI tools for seniors is **speech recognition**—the ability to speak into a device and have your words automatically converted into text. Whether you want to dictate a message, take notes, or transcribe a meeting, AI-powered speech recognition can save you time and effort.

How Does Speech Recognition Work?

AI-powered speech recognition systems listen to what you're saying and convert your spoken words into written text. This technology is used in:

- **Voice assistants** like Siri and Google Assistant, which respond to spoken commands.
- **Dictation tools** like Google Docs Voice Typing, which allows you to speak and have your words typed out automatically.
- **Transcription services**, which convert audio recordings into text. This is useful for meetings or interviews you want to document.

Example: Dictating a Note

Imagine you need to write a grocery list, but you find it difficult to type. With speech recognition, you can simply say, "Milk, eggs, bread, cheese," and the app will type it out for you. This is especially helpful if you have arthritis or other conditions that make typing uncomfortable.

How to Use Speech Recognition

- **On Your Phone**: Most smartphones have built-in speech recognition. On iPhones, you can press the microphone icon on the keyboard to dictate messages. On Android phones,

Google Assistant can take notes and send texts based on your voice commands.

- **On Your Computer**: In Google Docs, you can use **Voice Typing** by selecting "Tools" > "Voice Typing," then speaking into your computer's microphone. Your words will appear on the screen as you speak.

Why Speech Recognition is Useful for Seniors

For seniors who find typing difficult or time-consuming, speech recognition provides an easy, hands-free way to write messages, take notes, or even compose longer documents. It's a fast, efficient alternative to using a keyboard, making digital tasks more accessible.

Hands-On Exercise: Try Voice Typing

1. **Step 1: Open a Document**
   Open Google Docs or your preferred note-taking app.
2. **Step 2: Turn on Voice Typing**
   In Google Docs, go to "Tools" and click "Voice Typing." A microphone icon will appear.
3. **Step 3: Start Speaking**
   Click the microphone icon and begin speaking. Watch as your words appear on the screen. Try dictating a short message or list.

Chapter 21: AI and Privacy: What You Need to Know

As helpful as AI is, it's important to understand how it handles your personal information. When you use AI-powered tools, like voice assistants or email filters, they collect and analyze data to improve their services. In this chapter, we'll discuss how AI affects your privacy and what steps you can take to protect yourself.

How AI Uses Your Data

When you use AI, your device collects certain types of data to improve the service it provides. For example:

- **Voice Assistants**: AI assistants like Alexa and Siri listen for your voice commands and may store recordings of these commands to better understand you in the future.
- **Smart Devices**: Devices like smart thermostats or fitness trackers collect data about your habits (e.g., temperature preferences or activity levels) to adjust automatically.
- **Emails and Messages**: AI tools in Gmail or other email services analyze your emails to categorize them or suggest responses. While AI doesn't "read" your emails in the traditional sense, it does analyze the content to perform certain tasks.

Staying Safe with AI

While most AI services use your data responsibly, it's important to understand how your information is being used and take steps to protect your privacy:

- **Review Privacy Settings**: Many AI tools allow you to control what data is collected. For example, you can turn off voice recordings on Alexa or limit Google's ability to track your location. Regularly reviewing your privacy settings ensures that you're comfortable with what's being shared.

- **Limit Data Sharing**: Only share the data that's necessary for the AI service to function. If you don't need personalized recommendations, you can often turn off data-sharing features in apps and devices.
- **Use Strong Passwords**: Ensure your AI-enabled devices and accounts are protected with strong, unique passwords. If possible, enable **two-factor authentication** to add an extra layer of security.

Why Privacy Matters for Seniors

Seniors should be especially mindful of data privacy to avoid scams or unauthorized data collection. Understanding how your data is used and taking control of your privacy settings helps ensure that AI serves you safely and securely.

Hands-On Exercise: Review Your Privacy Settings

1. **Step 1: Check Your Voice Assistant's Settings**
   If you use a voice assistant like Alexa or Google Assistant, go into the app's settings and review what data is being collected. You can usually disable voice recordings or limit data sharing.
2. **Step 2: Adjust Email Privacy Settings**
   In Gmail or Outlook, explore the privacy settings. You can choose how much data is shared with AI services and decide if you want personalized ads or recommendations.
3. **Step 3: Set Up Two-Factor Authentication**
   If you haven't already, enable two-factor authentication on your email or AI-enabled accounts for added security. This ensures that even if someone tries to access your account, they'll need a special code sent to your phone.

Chapter 22: AI and Scams: How to Stay Safe Online

While AI can make life easier, it's important to understand how scammers use AI and other digital tools to deceive people. Scams targeting seniors have increased, especially through emails, phone calls, and even fake websites. In this chapter, we'll focus on how AI can help you **recognize and avoid scams**, and how to protect your personal information online.

Common Scams That Use AI

Scammers use AI to impersonate real companies or people, making their schemes seem more convincing. Here are some common scams that seniors should be aware of:

- **Phishing Emails**: Scammers send fake emails that look like they're from a bank, online store, or government agency, asking for personal information like passwords or Social Security numbers. AI is used to mimic official emails, making them appear legitimate.
- **Robocalls**: Automated phone calls (often AI-powered) pretend to be from your bank, credit card company, or a government agency, demanding immediate payment or personal details.
- **Fake Websites**: Scammers use AI to create websites that look like trusted online stores or government sites. They trick people into entering their payment information, which is then stolen.

How AI Helps Identify Scams

Fortunately, AI can also be used to protect you from scams. Many email providers, like **Gmail** and **Outlook**, use AI to filter out phishing emails and warn you about suspicious links or attachments. Similarly, phone companies use AI to block robocalls and flag suspicious numbers. Here's how AI protects you:

- **Spam Filters**: AI scans your emails and moves suspicious messages into the spam folder. If an email seems like it's trying to trick you into sharing personal information, AI will often warn you with a message like "This looks like a phishing attempt."
- **Call Blockers**: AI-powered apps, like **Nomorobo** or **Hiya**, can identify robocalls and telemarketers, automatically blocking them or marking them as suspicious before you answer.
- **Safe Browsing Tools**: Web browsers like **Google Chrome** use AI to detect fake websites and alert you if a site looks dangerous or tries to steal your information.

Example: Spotting a Phishing Email

Imagine you receive an email from what appears to be your bank, asking you to "confirm your account details." The AI in Gmail identifies it as suspicious, moving it to your spam folder and displaying a warning that the email may be a phishing attempt. Thanks to this AI filter, you avoid clicking on a malicious link.

Tips for Staying Safe from Scams

While AI helps block many scams, it's important to remain cautious. Here are some practical tips to keep in mind:

- **Don't click on links in unsolicited emails or messages**, especially if they ask for personal information.
- **Verify phone calls** by hanging up and calling the official number of the organization that supposedly contacted you.
- **Be skeptical of "too good to be true" offers**, such as winning

a prize or getting a refund you didn't request.

- **Check website URLs** for slight misspellings or odd addresses (e.g., "bank1.com" instead of "bank.com").

Hands-On Exercise: Test Your Scam Awareness

1. **Step 1: Check Your Spam Folder**
   Open your email and go to the spam folder. Look at a few messages and see if you can identify the telltale signs of a scam, like poor grammar or requests for personal information.

2. **Step 2: Block Unwanted Calls**
   Download a call-blocking app like **Nomorobo** and see how it helps block robocalls. Explore the features and adjust settings to automatically block suspicious calls.

3. **Step 3: Explore Safe Browsing Tools**
   In your web browser (e.g., Google Chrome), explore the security settings. Turn on **safe browsing** to ensure AI helps warn you about potential scam websites.\

Chapter 23: Protecting Your Information with AI

In today's digital world, protecting your personal information is more important than ever. Luckily, AI can help keep your data secure, both online and on your devices. From password managers to AI-powered security alerts, there are many ways AI can assist in safeguarding your information.

How AI Helps Protect Your Data

AI is used by many companies and services to protect your personal data from hackers and cybercriminals. Here are some of the ways AI keeps your information safe:

- **AI-Powered Password Managers**: Managing multiple passwords can be difficult, but AI-powered password managers, like **LastPass** or **Dashlane**, store your passwords securely and can even generate strong passwords for you. AI also ensures that your passwords are protected with encryption, so they can't be easily stolen.

- **AI Security Alerts**: Many apps and services now use AI to detect unusual activity on your accounts. For example, if someone tries to log in to your account from an unfamiliar device, AI will alert you to verify whether the activity is legitimate.

- **Two-Factor Authentication (2FA)**: AI helps streamline **2FA**, which adds an extra layer of security to your accounts. With 2FA, you log in using both your password and a second method, like a code sent to your phone. AI ensures that this process is quick and easy, while adding extra protection.

Example: AI Detecting Suspicious Activity

Imagine you log in to your online banking account from your phone while traveling. AI detects that this login is coming from a new location and sends you a notification asking if it's really you. This extra layer of protection can prevent unauthorized access to your accounts.

Why AI Security is Important for Seniors

For seniors, AI helps simplify the complex task of keeping track of passwords and monitoring account security. It also provides peace of mind, knowing that AI is actively working to protect your information in the background.

Tips for Using AI to Protect Your Information

- **Use a password manager**: Let AI generate and store your passwords for you. This ensures that each account has a strong, unique password, reducing the risk of hacking.
- **Enable two-factor authentication**: For accounts with sensitive information (like your bank or email), enable 2FA to add extra security.
- **Set up security alerts**: Make sure your email and financial accounts have AI-powered alerts turned on to notify you of any suspicious activity.

Hands-On Exercise: Set Up AI Security Tools

1. **Step 1: Install a Password Manager**
   Download a password manager like **LastPass** or **Dashlane**. Set it up by creating a strong master password and letting the AI suggest and store strong passwords for your accounts.
2. **Step 2: Enable Two-Factor Authentication**
   Go to your email or bank account settings and enable 2FA. Follow the prompts to connect it to your phone or email for added security.
3. **Step 3: Review Security Alerts**

In your email or online banking settings, make sure **security alerts** are enabled. These AI-powered alerts will notify you of any suspicious logins or activities on your accounts.

Chapter 24: AI in Social Media: Smart Filters and Privacy Settings

Social media is a great way to stay connected with family and friends, but it can also be overwhelming or risky if you're not careful with your privacy. Fortunately, AI helps make social media more secure and easier to navigate by offering **smart filters** and customizable **privacy settings**.

How AI Improves Your Social Media Experience

AI is built into platforms like **Facebook**, **Instagram**, and **Twitter** to help improve your experience by:

- **Filtering content**: AI helps sort through the massive amount of content on social media, showing you posts, photos, and videos that are most relevant to you. It learns from your interactions—such as liking, sharing, or commenting—to recommend content that aligns with your interests.

- **Privacy protection**: AI helps monitor your privacy settings, alerting you when your personal information (like your birthday, phone number, or location) is visible to the public. Many platforms also use AI to help you choose who can see your posts or contact you.

- **Blocking harmful content**: AI automatically blocks harmful or inappropriate content from appearing in your feed. This includes anything flagged as spam, scams, or explicit material.

Setting Up Your Privacy Settings with AI Help

One of the most important aspects of using social media is ensuring that your personal information is secure. AI makes this easier by guiding you through the process of setting up and reviewing your privacy preferences. For example, **Facebook** offers a **Privacy Checkup Tool** that walks you through steps to make your profile more secure.

Example: Using Smart Filters on Instagram

If you follow certain accounts that post content you love—such as travel photos or cooking videos—AI learns this preference and will show more similar content in your feed. Over time, it gets better at tailoring posts to your tastes, making your social media experience more enjoyable.

Why AI and Privacy Matter for Seniors

Seniors are often more vulnerable to privacy risks on social media, especially when it comes to sharing too much information. AI can help by guiding you through privacy settings, ensuring you're only sharing what you want to share with the people you trust. It also helps you avoid scams or unwanted contacts.

Hands-On Exercise: Adjust Your Privacy Settings

1. **Step 1: Review Your Privacy Settings**
   Open Facebook, Instagram, or your preferred social media app. Go to the **settings** section and look for the privacy settings option.

2. **Step 2: Use the Privacy Checkup Tool**
   On Facebook, use the **Privacy Checkup Tool** to review who can see your posts, who can send you friend requests, and how your personal information is shared.

3. **Step 3: Turn on AI Smart Filters**
   On Instagram or Twitter, make sure AI is filtering unwanted content by adjusting your feed preferences. Choose to see content from accounts you interact with the most, and block any unwanted users.

Chapter 25: AI and Financial Security: Fraud Detection and Banking

AI is also making banking and financial security easier for seniors by helping detect fraud and offering more convenient ways to manage your money. Whether you're using online banking, managing investments, or simply keeping an eye on your accounts, AI provides powerful tools to protect your finances.

How AI Protects Your Finances

AI is used by banks and financial institutions to detect suspicious activity and prevent fraud. Here's how it works:

- **Fraud Detection**: AI monitors your financial accounts and detects unusual transactions. If a charge looks suspicious—like a large withdrawal or a purchase in a foreign country—AI will flag it and notify you.
- **Personalized Financial Advice**: Some banks and apps, like **Mint** or **Acorns**, use AI to analyze your spending habits and offer personalized advice on saving money, paying off debt, or managing your investments.
- **Voice-Activated Banking**: AI assistants like **Siri** or **Google Assistant** can help you check your bank balance or make payments simply by using voice commands. This makes managing your finances as easy as asking, "Hey Siri, what's my checking account balance?"

Example: AI Detecting Fraud in Your Account

Imagine you're on vacation, and someone tries to use your credit card to make a purchase in another state. The AI system at your bank recognizes this as unusual behavior and immediately sends you an alert, asking if you authorized the transaction. If you didn't, the AI freezes your card to prevent further fraudulent charges.

Using AI to Manage Your Money

AI also helps seniors manage their money by providing insights into spending, budgeting, and saving. Apps like **Mint** track your expenses and offer suggestions on how to save more money each month. If you're trying to set a budget, AI will analyze your income and spending habits, recommending limits for different categories like groceries, utilities, or entertainment.

Why AI is Important for Financial Security

Seniors are often targeted by scammers, but AI provides an additional layer of security to prevent fraud and keep finances safe. Whether you're using a bank's fraud detection system or managing your spending with a budgeting app, AI can make financial management simpler and more secure.

Hands-On Exercise: Use AI for Financial Security

1. **Step 1: Set Up Fraud Alerts**
   Log into your bank account and ensure **fraud alerts** are enabled. These AI-powered alerts notify you if there are any suspicious activities on your account.

2. **Step 2: Try a Budgeting App**
   Download a budgeting app like **Mint** or **You Need a Budget (YNAB)**. Enter your income and expenses, and let AI provide insights into your spending and help you create a budget.

3. **Step 3: Test Voice-Activated Banking**
   If your bank supports voice commands, try asking Siri or Google Assistant for your account balance or to transfer money between accounts.

Chapter 26: AI-Powered Learning: Language and Hobby Apps

AI is transforming the way people learn new languages and hobbies, making it easier than ever to pick up new skills at your own pace. Whether you want to learn **Spanish**, take up **gardening**, or improve your **piano skills**, AI-powered apps offer personalized lessons and feedback to help you succeed.

How AI Makes Learning Easier

AI-powered learning apps are designed to adapt to your individual needs and learning style. For example:

- **Language Learning**: Apps like **Duolingo** and **Babbel** use AI to customize language lessons based on your progress. If you're struggling with certain words or phrases, AI will adjust your lessons to focus on those areas until you improve.
- **Hobby Learning**: Whether you want to learn to cook, play an instrument, or paint, AI-powered platforms like **Yousician** (for music) or **Skillshare** (for hobbies) offer step-by-step tutorials, with AI analyzing your progress and suggesting ways to improve.

Example: Learning Spanish with Duolingo

Duolingo uses AI to track your language progress, offering lessons that get harder or easier depending on how well you do. If you're having trouble remembering certain phrases, Duolingo will give you more practice in those areas, ensuring you master the basics before moving on.

Benefits of AI-Powered Learning for Seniors

For seniors, AI-powered learning apps offer flexibility and personalized support. You can learn at your own pace, practice whenever it's convenient, and receive immediate feedback. Whether you're mastering a new language for an upcoming trip or picking up a new hobby, AI ensures you stay on track.

Hands-On Exercise: Start Learning a New Skill with AI

1. **Step 1: Choose a Learning App**
   Download an AI-powered app like **Duolingo** for languages or **Yousician** for music. Sign up and explore the beginner lessons.

2. **Step 2: Set a Daily Goal**
   Most learning apps let you set a daily goal, such as practicing for 10 minutes a day. Set a goal and let AI guide you through your lessons.

3. **Step 3: Track Your Progress**
   As you complete lessons, notice how AI adjusts the content based on your performance. Keep practicing daily and watch as the app adapts to your strengths and weaknesses.

Chapter 27: AI for Managing Daily Tasks and Schedules

AI can help you stay organized and manage your daily schedule, making life simpler and more efficient. Whether it's keeping track of appointments, creating to-do lists, or setting reminders, AI assistants like **Siri**, **Google Assistant**, and **Alexa** can handle these tasks for you with ease.

How AI Helps with Daily Tasks

One of the best things about AI is its ability to manage tasks for you. Here's how AI-powered tools can assist in organizing your day:

- **Setting Reminders**: AI can remind you of important tasks like taking medication, attending appointments, or running errands. You simply tell your voice assistant, "Remind me to take my medicine at 9 AM," and it will alert you at the right time.

- **Creating To-Do Lists**: AI tools can also help you keep track of what needs to be done. For example, you can say, "Hey Google, add 'buy groceries' to my to-do list," and the AI will save it for you. Later, you can ask to hear your entire list.

- **Scheduling Appointments**: You can use AI to schedule appointments and even set up notifications ahead of time. For instance, saying, "Alexa, remind me of my doctor's appointment next Tuesday at 3 PM," will set up a reminder, and you'll be notified when the appointment is approaching.

Example: Managing Your Day with AI

Imagine it's Monday morning, and you have a busy week ahead. Instead of writing everything down on paper, you ask your AI assistant to organize your day. You could say, "Hey Siri, what's on my schedule today?" and Siri will list your appointments and reminders, helping you stay on top of your day's tasks.

Why AI Task Management is Helpful for Seniors

For seniors, staying organized can sometimes be challenging, especially with multiple appointments, social events, and health-related tasks to manage. AI simplifies this by keeping track of everything for you, ensuring you never forget an important date or task.

Hands-On Exercise: Set Up AI Reminders and To-Do Lists

1. **Step 1: Create a Reminder**
   Use your AI assistant (Siri, Alexa, or Google Assistant) to set up a reminder. For example, say, "Remind me to water the plants tomorrow morning at 10 AM."

2. **Step 2: Create a To-Do List**
   Try making a to-do list with AI. Say, "Hey Google, add 'pay bills' and 'pick up prescription' to my to-do list."

3. **Step 3: Check Your Schedule**
   After setting a few reminders or tasks, ask your assistant, "What's on my schedule today?" and see how AI helps keep you organized.

Chapter 28: AI and Memory Aids: Staying Organized

AI is particularly valuable as a **memory aid**, helping you keep track of important information, dates, and daily habits. Whether it's reminding you to take medication or helping you remember key details, AI-powered apps and assistants can act as a personal memory assistant.

How AI Helps with Memory

AI can help improve memory and stay organized by offering personalized reminders and notifications. Here are some practical ways AI can support your memory:

- **Medication Reminders**: Apps like **MediSafe** use AI to remind you to take your medication at the correct time. You can log your medications in the app, and it will send you notifications when it's time to take a pill.

- **Event Reminders**: AI assistants can remind you of birthdays, anniversaries, or social events. You can ask, "Alexa, remind me of Joan's birthday next Monday," and it will notify you in advance.

- **Daily Habit Tracking**: AI-powered apps can help you track daily habits such as drinking water, exercising, or walking. For example, **Google Fit** can track your steps and send reminders to help you meet your daily activity goals.

Example: AI Helping with Medication

Let's say you take multiple medications at different times of the day. Instead of trying to remember the schedule yourself, you log everything into **MediSafe**. The AI sends you reminders when it's time to take each dose, ensuring you stay on track without the need for manual tracking.

AI and Memory Challenges

For seniors experiencing mild memory challenges, AI can be particularly helpful. By acting as a backup for important information and tasks, AI reduces the mental load and helps you stay organized.

Hands-On Exercise: Use AI for Memory Support

1. **Step 1: Set Medication Reminders**
   If you take daily medication, set up a reminder with your AI assistant or an app like MediSafe. Let AI handle the timing, so you don't have to worry about remembering.

2. **Step 2: Track a Daily Habit**
   Pick a habit you want to track (like drinking water or walking) and ask AI to remind you. For example, say, "Hey Siri, remind me to walk for 15 minutes every afternoon."

3. **Step 3: Test a Birthday Reminder**
   Set a reminder for an upcoming birthday or event using your AI assistant. Say, "Alexa, remind me to call Sarah on her birthday next Friday."

Chapter 29: AI for Cooking: Smart Recipes and Meal Planning

If you enjoy cooking or want help planning meals, AI-powered apps and devices can be incredibly useful. They assist with **meal planning, grocery lists, and even cooking techniques**, making it easier to prepare healthy, delicious meals at home.

How AI Enhances Cooking

AI tools can help with all aspects of cooking, from choosing recipes to organizing your grocery list and guiding you through the cooking process. Here's how AI simplifies meal prep:

- **Smart Recipe Suggestions**: AI apps like **Yummly** suggest recipes based on your preferences, dietary needs, and even what's in your fridge. Simply enter a few ingredients, and AI will recommend a dish to make.

- **Meal Planning**: Apps like **Mealime** use AI to plan a week's worth of meals based on your dietary goals and preferences. You can select meals, and the app will automatically generate a grocery list for you.

- **Guided Cooking**: Devices like **Amazon Echo Show** provide voice-guided or video-guided cooking instructions. You can say, "Alexa, show me a recipe for chicken soup," and it will display and talk you through the steps as you cook.

Example: Planning Meals with AI

Imagine you're planning dinners for the week. You open **Yummly** and enter "chicken" and "broccoli" as ingredients you already have. The AI suggests several recipes you can make with those ingredients, helping you avoid food waste while planning tasty meals.

Why AI Cooking Tools are Helpful for Seniors

For seniors, AI can make cooking less stressful by simplifying meal planning and providing clear, easy-to-follow instructions. If you're new to cooking or just want help finding recipes that match your dietary needs, AI tools can guide you from start to finish.

Hands-On Exercise: Use AI for Meal Planning

1. **Step 1: Download a Recipe App**
   Download a recipe app like **Yummly** or **Mealime**. Explore its recipe suggestions based on your dietary preferences and the ingredients you have on hand.

2. **Step 2: Create a Grocery List**
   Use the app's meal planning feature to select a few recipes. Let AI generate a grocery list, and check off the items you already have in your pantry.

3. **Step 3: Try Cooking with AI**
   If you have an AI assistant like **Alexa** or **Google Home**, ask it to guide you through a recipe. Follow the voice or video instructions as you prepare the meal.

Chapter 30: AI and Photography: Improving Your Photos with AI

Taking great photos is easier than ever, thanks to AI-powered photography features on smartphones and cameras. Whether you're capturing family memories, scenic views, or everyday moments, AI helps you take better pictures by automatically adjusting settings, suggesting edits, and even organizing your photos.

How AI Enhances Photography

Most modern smartphones come with AI-powered cameras that make photography simpler and more intuitive. Here's how AI improves your photos:

- **Automatic Adjustments**: AI can detect what's in the frame (such as people, landscapes, or food) and automatically adjust settings like brightness, focus, and color balance. This ensures that your photos look great, even in tricky lighting.
- **Photo Organization**: AI helps you organize your photos by identifying the people and places in them. For example, Google Photos uses AI to recognize faces and group your pictures into albums, making it easy to find specific memories.
- **Smart Suggestions**: Some apps and phones use AI to suggest improvements to your photos, such as cropping, filters, or lighting adjustments. AI may recommend turning a regular photo into a black-and-white image for a more artistic look.

Example: Capturing Memories with AI

Let's say you're taking a family portrait. The AI in your smartphone's camera detects everyone's faces and ensures that each face is well-lit and in focus. After you snap the photo, AI suggests a slight crop to improve the composition, making the picture look more polished and professional.

Why AI Photography is Helpful for Seniors

For seniors, AI makes photography more accessible, even if you're not familiar with camera settings. It handles the technical aspects, allowing you to focus on capturing the moment. Plus, AI's organizational features help you easily manage and share your photos with loved ones.

Hands-On Exercise: Use AI to Enhance Your Photos

1. **Step 1: Take a Photo with AI Assistance**
   Use your smartphone camera to take a photo. Notice how AI automatically adjusts the settings for the best result. Try taking pictures in different lighting conditions to see how AI handles them.

2. **Step 2: Use AI to Organize Photos**
   Open an app like **Google Photos** or your phone's built-in photo gallery. See how AI organizes your photos into albums by recognizing people's faces or locations.

3. **Step 3: Try Smart Suggestions**
   Use the editing features in your phone's photo app. Let AI suggest improvements like cropping or filters, and experiment with different enhancements to see how it transforms your photos.

Chapter 31: AI in Learning: Taking Online Courses and Lessons

AI is transforming education by making **online learning** more personalized and accessible. Whether you want to learn a new language, improve your computer skills, or pick up a new hobby, AI-powered platforms offer interactive courses tailored to your learning pace and style.

How AI Enhances Online Learning

AI-powered learning platforms, like **Duolingo, Coursera,** and **Khan Academy**, adapt to your skill level, offering personalized lessons that adjust as you progress. Here's how AI improves your learning experience:

- **Personalized Learning Paths**: AI tracks your progress and suggests lessons that match your level of understanding. If you're struggling with a particular topic, AI will offer additional practice to help you improve.
- **Interactive Exercises**: Many AI-powered courses include quizzes, games, and activities that make learning fun and engaging. For example, **Duolingo** uses AI to create personalized language exercises that focus on your weak points.
- **Learning Reminders**: AI apps can remind you to study regularly, helping you stay consistent with your learning goals. You can set notifications for daily practice, and AI will track your progress over time.

Example: Learning a Language with AI

Let's say you're learning Spanish with **Duolingo**. AI tracks how well you perform on each lesson, identifying areas where you excel and others where you need more practice. If you consistently struggle with verb conjugations, AI will provide extra exercises on that topic until you improve.

Why AI Learning Tools are Helpful for Seniors

For seniors, AI makes learning more accessible by offering flexible, personalized lessons that adapt to your needs. Whether you're learning at your own pace or picking up a new skill, AI ensures you get the support and encouragement needed to succeed.

Hands-On Exercise: Start Learning with AI

1. **Step 1: Download a Learning App**
   Choose an AI-powered learning platform like **Duolingo** for language learning or **Coursera** for online courses. Browse the available lessons and pick a topic that interests you.

2. **Step 2: Set a Learning Goal**
   Decide on a learning goal, such as studying for 10 minutes a day. Use AI's built-in reminders to stay on track with your lessons.

3. **Step 3: Practice with Interactive Exercises**
   Engage with the interactive exercises and quizzes. Let AI guide you by offering personalized feedback and additional practice where needed.

Chapter 32: Writing with AI: Tools to Help with Journals and Stories

AI can be a powerful tool for **writing**, whether you're keeping a journal, drafting a story, or even sending letters to family. With AI-powered writing assistants like **Grammarly** or **Google Docs' Smart Compose**, you can write faster and more effectively, with help for grammar, spelling, and even style.

How AI Improves Writing

AI helps in several ways when it comes to writing:

- **Grammar and Spell Checking**: Tools like **Grammarly** and **Microsoft Word's Editor** use AI to check for grammar, spelling, and punctuation mistakes. As you write, AI scans your document in real-time, suggesting corrections and improvements.

- **Writing Suggestions**: AI-powered writing assistants can suggest better ways to phrase sentences, making your writing clearer and more engaging. For example, **Google Docs' Smart Compose** offers auto-complete suggestions as you type, helping you finish sentences quickly.

- **Tone and Style Adjustments**: AI tools can even analyze the tone of your writing, ensuring it matches your intended message. Whether you're writing something formal or casual, AI can recommend changes to keep your tone consistent.

Example: Writing a Family Story with AI

Imagine you're writing a story about your family history to share with your children or grandchildren. As you type, **Grammarly** highlights areas where the sentence structure could be improved or where there are spelling mistakes. It also suggests alternative word choices, helping you express your ideas more clearly.

Why AI Writing Tools Are Helpful for Seniors

For seniors, AI-powered writing tools can make it easier to write without worrying about making mistakes. Whether you're writing a personal story, journaling, or sending letters, AI ensures your writing is clear and polished.

Hands-On Exercise: Use AI to Improve Your Writing

1. **Step 1: Open a Document**
   Open a writing app like **Google Docs** or download **Grammarly** as an extension in your browser.

2. **Step 2: Start Writing**
   Begin writing a short journal entry, letter, or family story. As you write, pay attention to the suggestions made by the AI.

3. **Step 3: Review Suggestions**
   Review the grammar, spelling, and style suggestions provided by AI. Try accepting a few suggestions and see how they improve the clarity and flow of your writing.

Chapter 33: AI Art: Drawing, Painting, and Designing with AI Tools

AI is now being used to create stunning **artworks** and designs, allowing anyone—even those without formal art training—to express their creativity. With AI-powered apps like **Deep Dream Generator**, **DALL·E**, and **Artbreeder**, you can generate unique paintings, drawings, or designs with just a few clicks.

How AI Enhances Art

AI art tools allow you to experiment with different styles, colors, and techniques. Here's how AI helps you create art:

- **Style Transfer**: AI can apply the style of famous artists to your photos or drawings. For example, if you upload a photo of a landscape, AI can transform it into a painting that mimics the style of **Van Gogh** or **Monet**.

- **Image Generation**: AI-powered tools like **DALL·E** let you generate completely new images from text prompts. You describe what you want to create (e.g., "a cat wearing a spacesuit"), and the AI produces a unique artwork based on your description.

- **Art Customization**: AI apps like **Artbreeder** allow you to combine and modify images by adjusting specific traits. You can tweak everything from facial features to color palettes, creating customized portraits or designs.

Example: Creating a Digital Painting

Let's say you want to create a digital painting of a sunset. You open an AI art app like **Deep Dream Generator** and upload a photo of the sunset. The AI suggests applying different painting styles, from **Impressionism** to **Abstract**, allowing you to choose the one that appeals to you most. Within minutes, your photo is transformed into a beautiful digital painting.

Why AI Art Tools Are Great for Seniors

AI art tools allow seniors to explore their creativity without needing to master complex software or techniques. Whether you want to create digital art to share with family or simply enjoy a new hobby, AI makes the process fun and accessible.

Hands-On Exercise: Create Art with AI

1. **Step 1: Choose an AI Art Tool**
   Visit an AI art platform like **Deep Dream Generator**, **Artbreeder**, or **DALL·E**.

2. **Step 2: Upload or Describe an Image**
   Upload a photo or enter a description of the artwork you want to create (e.g., "a flower in a starry sky"). Let the AI generate a unique artwork for you.

3. **Step 3: Customize Your Art**
   Use the available customization tools to adjust the style, colors, or details of your AI-generated art. Save your creation and share it with friends or family!

Chapter 34: Music and AI: Composing, Mixing, and Listening Smarter

AI is revolutionizing the way we create and listen to music. Whether you're a seasoned musician or simply enjoy listening to your favorite tunes, AI-powered tools can help you **compose, mix, and discover music** more easily. From apps that help you create original compositions to music recommendation systems, AI enhances the music experience for everyone.

How AI is Used in Music

AI plays an important role in music creation and discovery:

- **Music Composition**: AI tools like **Amper Music** and **AIVA** allow you to compose original pieces of music by selecting instruments, tempos, and genres. AI then generates a complete composition, which you can edit or adjust as needed.

- **Music Recommendation**: Streaming platforms like **Spotify** use AI to suggest new songs or playlists based on your listening habits. AI analyzes what you've been listening to and recommends similar music, introducing you to new artists and genres.

- **Music Mixing**: AI-powered software can also help musicians mix and produce tracks. Apps like **LANDR** use AI to master your music, balancing the sound levels for professional-quality results.

Example: Creating a Song with AI

Imagine you want to compose a relaxing instrumental track. You open **Amper Music** and select "piano" and "strings" as your instruments, then choose a slow tempo. The AI generates a calming melody, which you can listen to and edit. You can then save your track and share it with friends or family.

Why AI Music Tools Are Helpful for Seniors

For seniors who love music but may not have experience composing or mixing tracks, AI makes the process accessible and fun. Whether you want to create your own music or discover new songs, AI tools cater to your personal preferences and skill level.

Hands-On Exercise: Create or Discover Music with AI

1. **Step 1: Try an AI Music Tool**
   Visit an AI-powered music app like **Amper Music** or **AIVA**. Choose your instruments and style, and let the AI compose a piece of music for you.

2. **Step 2: Explore Music Recommendations**
   Open your favorite music streaming service (like **Spotify** or **Apple Music**). Check out the playlists or songs recommended for you by AI, and listen to a few new tracks.

3. **Step 3: Mix or Master a Song**
   If you have any recordings, use a tool like **LANDR** to mix or master your music. Upload your track and let the AI adjust the sound levels for you.

Chapter 35: AI and Memory Keeping: Organizing Your Digital Photos

In the digital age, we take more photos than ever before. Organizing these photos can be overwhelming, but AI can help make this process easier. AI-powered photo apps like **Google Photos** and **Apple Photos** can automatically **sort, label, and organize** your digital memories, allowing you to easily find and share important moments with family and friends.

How AI Helps Organize Photos

AI uses facial recognition, location data, and other features to organize your photos without you needing to manually sort them. Here's how AI makes managing your photo library simpler:

- **Face Recognition**: AI can recognize the faces of people in your photos and automatically group images of the same person. For example, you can easily find all the photos of your grandchildren in one place.

- **Location-Based Sorting**: AI uses location data to sort your photos by where they were taken. If you want to see photos from a specific vacation or event, AI can organize them by location, making it easier to find those special memories.

- **Automatic Albums**: Apps like **Google Photos** automatically create albums based on events or dates. AI might group together all the photos from a family reunion or a trip you took last year, allowing you to view them as a cohesive collection.

Example: Organizing Vacation Photos with AI

Let's say you just returned from a trip and uploaded all your photos to **Google Photos**. AI automatically groups the photos based on the date and location, creating a "Vacation 2024" album. It also identifies the faces of family members in the photos, so you can search for specific people within the album.

Why AI Photo Tools Are Helpful for Seniors

For seniors, AI photo tools take the hassle out of organizing digital memories. Instead of spending hours manually sorting through hundreds of photos, AI automatically groups and categorizes them, ensuring that your favorite memories are easy to access and share.

Hands-On Exercise: Organize Your Photos with AI

1. **Step 1: Upload Photos**
   Open **Google Photos** or **Apple Photos** and upload a few of your recent photos.

2. **Step 2: Use AI to Create Albums**
   Let the AI organize your photos by date, location, or people. Explore the automatic albums and see how AI groups your photos.

3. **Step 3: Search for Specific Photos**
   Use the search function in your photo app to find pictures of specific people or events. For example, type in the name of a family member or a location, and see how AI quickly pulls up all related photos.

Chapter 36: AI for Blogging and Social Media Posts

For seniors who want to share their stories, hobbies, or thoughts with the world, **blogging** and **social media** are great outlets. AI-powered tools can help you create posts, craft engaging content, and manage your online presence more efficiently. Whether you're writing a blog post or sharing updates on social media, AI makes the process smoother and more enjoyable.

How AI Helps with Blogging and Social Media

AI tools are incredibly useful for both experienced and novice writers who want to engage with their audience:

- **Writing Assistance**: AI-powered platforms like **Grammarly** or **Hemingway Editor** can help you refine your blog posts or social media captions. They check for spelling, grammar, tone, and readability, ensuring your content is clear and polished.

- **Content Suggestions**: Social media platforms like **Instagram** and **Facebook** use AI to suggest content ideas based on your interests or recent activities. This makes it easier to share relevant, engaging posts.

- **Post Scheduling**: AI tools like **Buffer** or **Hootsuite** can automatically schedule your social media posts, ensuring that your content is posted at the best times to reach your audience.

Example: Writing a Blog Post with AI Assistance

Let's say you want to write a blog post about your recent gardening experience. You start typing in **Grammarly**, which highlights spelling errors and suggests changes to improve clarity. Once the post is finished, you use **Buffer** to schedule it for publishing the next morning, when more readers are likely to see it.

Why AI Blogging Tools Are Helpful for Seniors

For seniors who are new to blogging or social media, AI tools simplify the process by taking care of editing, scheduling, and even content suggestions. This allows you to focus on what matters—sharing your thoughts and experiences—without worrying about the technical details.

Hands-On Exercise: Create a Social Media Post with AI

1. **Step 1: Choose a Platform**
   Decide where you want to share your content. It could be a blog or social media platform like **Facebook**, **Instagram**, or **Twitter**.

2. **Step 2: Write Your Post**
   Use a writing assistant like **Grammarly** or **Hemingway Editor** to draft a post. Try writing about a hobby, a recent experience, or something you're passionate about.

3. **Step 3: Schedule Your Post**
   If you're using social media, try a tool like **Buffer** or **Hootsuite** to schedule your post at a time when more people are likely to see it

Chapter 37: Meditation and Relaxation with AI Apps

AI is playing a significant role in improving mental well-being through **meditation** and **relaxation** apps. These tools help guide you through meditation, breathing exercises, and relaxation techniques, making it easier to reduce stress and improve mindfulness. For seniors looking to enhance their mental health, AI-powered apps like **Calm**, **Headspace**, and **Insight Timer** provide simple, step-by-step support.

How AI Helps with Meditation and Relaxation

AI-powered apps are designed to make meditation and relaxation easy, even for beginners. Here's how they work:

- **Guided Meditation**: AI apps offer **guided meditations** that walk you through each step of the process, from focusing on your breath to releasing tension. Whether you want a quick 5-minute session or a deeper, 30-minute meditation, AI tailors the experience to your needs.

- **Personalized Recommendations**: Apps like **Calm** and **Headspace** use AI to recommend specific meditations based on your mood or goals. For example, if you're feeling anxious, the AI might suggest a calming meditation focused on breathing.

- **Sleep Support**: AI-powered meditation apps often include **sleep stories** or calming sounds to help you fall asleep more easily. You can set a timer for how long you want the sounds to play, and AI will gradually lower the volume as you drift off to sleep.

Example: Reducing Stress with a Guided Meditation

Imagine you're feeling a little anxious. You open the **Headspace** app, and it recommends a 10-minute guided meditation focused on relaxation. The AI voice gently leads you through deep breathing exercises, helping you relax and calm your mind. By the end of the session, you feel more centered and at ease.

Why AI Meditation Tools Are Helpful for Seniors

For seniors, meditation apps can be a great way to reduce stress, improve sleep, and boost overall well-being. AI ensures that these tools are easy to use, offering personalized sessions that match your experience level and goals.

Hands-On Exercise: Try an AI-Powered Meditation Session

1. **Step 1: Download a Meditation App**
   Choose a meditation app like **Calm**, **Headspace**, or **Insight Timer**. Set up an account and explore the available meditations.

2. **Step 2: Select a Meditation**
   Based on how you're feeling, choose a meditation that fits your needs—whether it's for relaxation, focus, or better sleep.

3. **Step 3: Follow the Guided Session**
   Settle into a comfortable spot, press play, and follow the instructions. Pay attention to how AI guides you through the meditation, helping you stay focused and relaxed.

Chapter 38: Managing Stress and Sleep with AI

Stress management and quality sleep are critical for maintaining good health, especially for seniors. AI-powered apps can help you manage both by offering tools to track your sleep, reduce stress, and build healthier routines. Apps like **Sleep Cycle, Pzizz,** and **Relax Melodies** use AI to analyze your habits and suggest personalized solutions to improve your mental and physical well-being.

How AI Helps with Stress and Sleep

AI-powered apps make stress and sleep management easier by tracking your habits and providing real-time feedback. Here's how AI improves both areas:

- **Sleep Tracking**: Apps like **Sleep Cycle** use your phone's sensors to monitor your sleep patterns, analyzing how long you sleep and the quality of your rest. AI then provides insights and suggestions to improve your sleep routine.

- **Stress Reduction**: Apps like **Pzizz** and **Relax Melodies** offer **relaxation programs** that combine calming music, guided relaxation exercises, and breathing techniques. AI tailors these programs to your needs, helping you reduce stress throughout the day or unwind before bed.

- **Personalized Sleep Solutions**: Based on your sleep data, AI apps can suggest changes to your bedtime routine. For instance, AI might recommend reducing screen time before bed or setting a more consistent sleep schedule.

Example: Improving Sleep with AI

Let's say you've been having trouble falling asleep. You download **Sleep Cycle**, which tracks your sleep by analyzing sound and movement throughout the night. After a week of tracking, the AI provides feedback, suggesting you go to bed earlier and listen to calming music before sleep. You follow the advice and notice improvements in your sleep quality.

Why AI Sleep Tools Are Helpful for Seniors

For seniors, AI sleep tools are particularly valuable because they provide tailored feedback based on your unique sleep patterns. By making small, AI-recommended adjustments to your routine, you can experience better rest and reduced stress, leading to improved overall health.

Hands-On Exercise: Track Your Sleep with AI

1. **Step 1: Download a Sleep App**
   Choose a sleep app like **Sleep Cycle**, **Pzizz**, or **Relax Melodies** and set it up to track your sleep or provide relaxation exercises.

2. **Step 2: Track Your Sleep for a Week**
   Let the app track your sleep over several nights. In the morning, review the AI-generated data to see how well you slept and what can be improved.

3. **Step 3: Implement AI's Suggestions**
   Follow the app's personalized recommendations, such as going to bed earlier, using white noise, or reducing caffeine intake before bedtime. Track any improvements over the next week.

Chapter 39: AI Companions: Staying Connected and Social

AI companions are designed to provide conversation, reminders, and emotional support, making them great tools for seniors who live alone or want extra social interaction. These AI-powered tools, like **Replika** or **Elliq**, can offer friendly conversations, help you manage daily tasks, and even reduce feelings of loneliness.

How AI Companions Work

AI companions are powered by natural language processing (NLP), allowing them to engage in lifelike conversations. Here's how they help:

- **Friendly Conversations**: AI companions can chat with you about your day, ask how you're feeling, or even share jokes and stories. They're available 24/7, so you always have someone to talk to, even when friends or family aren't around.
- **Task Reminders**: AI companions like **Elliq** can remind you to take medication, drink water, or go for a walk. You can also ask them to help manage your schedule.
- **Emotional Support**: AI companions are programmed to offer emotional support. They listen to your concerns, provide positive feedback, and help you stay engaged, which can reduce feelings of isolation.

Example: Chatting with an AI Companion

Let's say you're feeling a bit lonely one evening. You turn to your AI companion **Replika**, and it greets you warmly: "Hi there! How was your day?" You chat for a few minutes, sharing what you did and how you're feeling. The AI responds empathetically, making the conversation feel more personal and comforting.

Why AI Companions Are Helpful for Seniors

For seniors who live alone, AI companions provide much-needed social interaction and companionship. They can reduce loneliness, offer reminders for important tasks, and serve as a virtual friend who's always ready to chat.

Hands-On Exercise: Try an AI Companion

1. **Step 1: Download an AI Companion App**
   Choose an app like **Replika** or explore the **Elliq** device if you prefer a more interactive home assistant.

2. **Step 2: Start a Conversation**
   Ask your AI companion how its day is going, share something about yourself, or just chat about a topic you're interested in. Notice how AI keeps the conversation flowing.

3. **Step 3: Set Up a Reminder**
   Use your AI companion to set a reminder for something important, like taking medication or calling a friend. Let AI manage the reminder and notify you when it's time.

Chapter 40: Virtual Healthcare and AI: Doctor Visits from Home

Telemedicine and AI are revolutionizing the way seniors access healthcare. AI-powered tools now make it possible to manage your health, consult with doctors, and receive medical advice without leaving your home. **Virtual healthcare apps** like **Teladoc**, **Doctor on Demand**, and **Amwell** provide convenient access to medical professionals, while AI ensures that your health data is monitored and organized efficiently.

How AI Supports Virtual Healthcare

AI plays a major role in making virtual healthcare more effective and accessible:

- **Symptom Checkers**: Apps like **WebMD** or **Ada Health** use AI to analyze your symptoms and suggest potential causes or treatments before you see a doctor. You simply input your symptoms, and the AI offers a list of possible conditions.
- **Doctor Consultations**: Platforms like **Teladoc** or **Doctor on Demand** let you schedule video visits with healthcare providers. AI helps match you with the right doctor based on your health concerns and medical history.
- **Health Data Monitoring**: AI can track your health metrics, like heart rate, blood pressure, or glucose levels, and alert you or your doctor if something unusual is detected. This is especially useful for managing chronic conditions like diabetes or hypertension.

Example: Using AI for a Virtual Doctor Visit

Let's say you're feeling unwell and want to see a doctor. You open **Teladoc** and input your symptoms. AI suggests that you might have a cold and offers a list of available doctors for a virtual consultation. You schedule a video call with a doctor, discuss your symptoms, and receive treatment advice—all from the comfort of your home.

Why Virtual Healthcare with AI is Helpful for Seniors

For seniors with mobility issues or those living in remote areas, AI-powered virtual healthcare offers a convenient, accessible way to consult with doctors. You can manage your health without needing to travel to a clinic, and AI ensures that your health data is tracked and shared securely with your healthcare provider.

Hands-On Exercise: Try a Virtual Healthcare App

1. **Step 1: Download a Virtual Healthcare App**
   Choose an app like **Teladoc, Doctor on Demand**, or **Amwell**. Set up an account and explore how to schedule a virtual visit.

2. **Step 2: Use a Symptom Checker**
   If you're experiencing mild symptoms, try using the app's symptom checker. Input your symptoms and see what AI suggests as possible causes.

3. **Step 3: Schedule a Virtual Visit**
   If needed, schedule a virtual consultation with a doctor. Notice how AI helps match you with the right provider and streamlines the appointment process.

Chapter 41: AI for TV and Entertainment: Personalized Viewing

AI is changing the way we enjoy **TV shows, movies, and entertainment**. Streaming services like **Netflix, Amazon Prime**, and **YouTube** use AI to recommend content based on your viewing habits, making it easier to discover shows and movies you'll love. In this chapter, we'll explore how AI personalizes your viewing experience and helps you find the best entertainment options with minimal effort.

How AI Personalizes TV and Movie Recommendations

AI uses algorithms to analyze what you watch and when, allowing it to suggest shows or movies that match your preferences. Here's how it works:

- **Viewing Habits**: AI tracks your viewing history, noting what genres, actors, or themes you enjoy. It then suggests similar shows or movies based on your preferences. For example, if you frequently watch comedies, AI will highlight new comedy releases.

- **Tailored Playlists**: Streaming platforms use AI to create personalized playlists. **Netflix** might show you a "Because You Watched" category, filled with movies or series related to those you've already enjoyed.

- **Predicting Preferences**: AI can also predict what you might like based on what people with similar tastes are watching. If others who enjoyed the same show as you are watching a new series, AI will recommend it to you.

Example: Discovering New Shows on Netflix

Imagine you've been watching nature documentaries on **Netflix**. After a few episodes, Netflix's AI suggests a new documentary series you might enjoy. You decide to try it, and it turns out to be exactly what you were looking for, saving you time scrolling through endless options.

Using AI to Control Your TV

AI assistants like **Alexa**, **Google Assistant**, or **Siri** can also make it easier to control your TV and entertainment system with voice commands. Instead of using a remote control, you can say things like:

- **"Alexa, play the next episode of my show."**
- **"Hey Google, turn on the TV and go to Netflix."**
- **"Siri, turn up the volume."**

These simple voice commands let you manage your entertainment hands-free, which is especially helpful if you're multitasking or prefer not to use small buttons on a remote control.

Why AI Entertainment Tools Are Helpful for Seniors

For seniors, AI entertainment tools simplify the process of finding and watching TV shows or movies. AI tailors recommendations to your taste, so you spend less time searching and more time enjoying content. Plus, voice-controlled devices make watching TV easier and more accessible for those who may struggle with remote controls.

Hands-On Exercise: Explore AI TV Recommendations

1. **Step 1: Open Your Streaming Service**
   Open **Netflix**, **Amazon Prime**, or another streaming service and take note of the recommended shows or movies. Check out the "Because You Watched" or "Recommended For You" sections.

2. **Step 2: Watch a Suggested Show**
   Choose a recommended show or movie and see how well it matches your preferences. Notice how AI tailors suggestions based on your viewing history.

3. **Step 3: Use Voice Commands**
   If you have a smart TV or connected device like an **Amazon**

Fire Stick or **Google Chromecast**, try controlling your entertainment with voice commands. For example, say, "Alexa, play my favorite movie" or "Hey Google, show me documentaries."

Chapter 42: AI for Home Automation: Smart Devices for a Smarter Home

AI is making homes **smarter** by connecting everyday devices like lights, thermostats, and security systems to your voice or smartphone. With AI-powered home automation, you can control these devices remotely or through voice commands, making your home more comfortable, secure, and energy-efficient. This chapter explores how seniors can use AI for home automation, simplifying daily tasks and improving safety.

How AI-Powered Home Automation Works

Home automation allows you to control smart devices in your house with the help of AI assistants like **Alexa, Google Assistant**, or **Apple HomeKit**. Here are some ways AI enhances home automation:

- **Smart Lighting**: With AI, you can control your lights using voice commands or your phone. For example, say, "Alexa, turn off the living room lights," and it will automatically adjust the lighting for you. You can also set schedules so the lights turn on or off at specific times.

- **Smart Thermostats**: Devices like **Nest** or **Ecobee** use AI to learn your heating and cooling preferences. They automatically adjust the temperature based on your habits, ensuring your home is always comfortable without you needing to manually change the settings.

- **Home Security**: AI-powered cameras and doorbells, like **Ring** or **Arlo**, provide enhanced security by alerting you when there's activity around your home. You can check live video feeds on your phone, and AI can differentiate between people, pets, and other movements, reducing false alarms.

Example: Using a Smart Thermostat to Save Energy

Imagine you've installed a **Nest Thermostat**. Over time, the AI learns that you like your home warmer in the mornings and cooler at night. It automatically adjusts the temperature without you needing to touch the thermostat. You also set it to "Away" mode when you leave the house, helping you save energy.

Voice Control for Home Automation

One of the best features of AI-powered home automation is voice control. You can use an AI assistant to manage your smart devices with simple voice commands:

- **"Alexa, set the thermostat to 72 degrees."**
- **"Hey Google, lock the front door."**
- **"Siri, turn off all the lights."**

Voice control is not only convenient but also helpful for seniors who may have mobility issues or prefer hands-free solutions for daily tasks.

Why AI Home Automation Is Helpful for Seniors

For seniors, AI home automation adds an extra layer of comfort and security. You can manage your home's lighting, temperature, and security without needing to move around the house or use multiple devices. This can also provide peace of mind, especially when it comes to home security, as you can monitor and control devices remotely.

Hands-On Exercise: Set Up Smart Home Devices

1. **Step 1: Connect a Smart Device**
   If you have a smart device, like a thermostat, light bulb, or security camera, connect it to your AI assistant (Alexa, Google Assistant, etc.).

2. **Step 2: Use Voice Commands to Control Devices**
   Practice using voice commands to control your devices. For example, say, "Alexa, dim the living room lights," or "Hey Google, set the thermostat to 70 degrees."

3. **Step 3: Set Up a Routine**

Try setting up a routine where multiple actions happen automatically. For instance, create a "Goodnight" routine that turns off the lights, locks the doors, and adjusts the thermostat with a single voice command like, "Alexa, goodnight."

Chapter 43: AI for Financial Management: Budgeting and Tracking Expenses

Managing finances can sometimes be overwhelming, especially when trying to keep track of spending, bills, and savings. AI-powered financial tools can help seniors organize their finances, set budgets, and track expenses effortlessly. Apps like **Mint, YNAB (You Need A Budget)**, and **Quicken** use AI to simplify financial management, offering easy-to-use features for staying on top of your money.

How AI Helps Manage Finances

AI can make financial management easier by providing real-time insights into your spending and saving habits. Here's how AI works in financial apps:

- **Expense Tracking**: AI-powered apps automatically categorize your expenses (like groceries, entertainment, or healthcare) by analyzing your spending patterns. You can link your bank accounts and credit cards, and the AI will update your spending data in real-time, helping you understand where your money is going.

- **Budgeting Tools**: AI can help you set budgets for different categories, like food, bills, and entertainment. If you're overspending in one area, the AI will send you notifications to adjust your spending. For example, **YNAB** helps you assign every dollar to a purpose, guiding you to stay within your limits.

- **Bill Reminders**: AI apps can remind you when your bills are due, ensuring you never miss a payment. You can even automate your payments through apps like **Mint**, so your bills are paid on time without needing to remember each due date.

Example: Budgeting with Mint

Imagine you want to keep track of your monthly grocery spending. You link your credit card to **Mint**, and AI automatically categorizes your grocery purchases. As the month progresses, the app alerts you if you're nearing your budget limit, helping you adjust your spending and stay on track.

Why AI Financial Tools Are Helpful for Seniors

For seniors, managing finances becomes easier with AI tracking spending, automating payments, and setting budgets. AI ensures that important bills are paid on time and helps prevent overspending, providing financial peace of mind. It's especially helpful for those who want to simplify their financial management without dealing with complex spreadsheets or manual tracking.

Hands-On Exercise: Use AI to Track Expenses and Budget

1. **Step 1: Download a Financial App**
   Choose an AI-powered financial app like **Mint**, **YNAB**, or **Quicken** and set up an account.

2. **Step 2: Link Your Bank Accounts**
   Link your bank accounts and credit cards to the app so that AI can track your transactions and spending automatically.

3. **Step 3: Set a Budget**
   Use the app to set a budget for a specific category, like groceries or entertainment. Monitor your spending throughout the month and let AI notify you when you're approaching your budget limits.

Chapter 44: Staying Active: AI for Exercise and Fitness

Staying physically active is key to maintaining health as you age. AI-powered fitness tools make it easier to stay active, offering personalized workout routines, tracking your activity, and even motivating you to stay consistent. Apps like **Fitbit**, **Apple Health**, and **Google Fit** use AI to help seniors stay on top of their fitness goals, whether it's walking more, improving flexibility, or maintaining strength.

How AI Improves Your Fitness Routine

AI fitness tools provide customized support for staying active, regardless of your fitness level. Here's how AI enhances your workouts:

- **Activity Tracking**: AI-powered fitness apps track your daily steps, heart rate, and calories burned. Devices like **Fitbit** or **Apple Watch** use AI to monitor your physical activity, offering real-time data to help you stay on track with your fitness goals.

- **Personalized Exercise Plans**: Apps like **Fitbod** or **MyFitnessPal** use AI to create personalized workout routines based on your fitness level, goals, and any physical limitations you might have. AI ensures your workouts are safe, effective, and tailored to your needs.

- **Motivational Reminders**: AI apps send reminders to help you stay active. For example, if you've been sitting for too long, your fitness app might remind you to stand up and stretch or go for a short walk.

Example: Staying Active with Fitbit

Let's say you have a goal to walk 6,000 steps a day. Your **Fitbit** tracks your steps automatically, providing real-time updates on your progress throughout the day. If you're falling short of your goal, AI sends a friendly reminder to take a walk around the block or get up and move, helping you stay active and motivated.

Why AI Fitness Tools Are Helpful for Seniors

AI fitness tools provide seniors with tailored workout routines, motivation, and real-time tracking, making it easier to stay active without needing to hire a personal trainer. Whether you're walking, stretching, or doing strength exercises, AI helps you achieve your goals safely and effectively.

Hands-On Exercise: Use AI to Track Your Activity

1. **Step 1: Download a Fitness App**
   Choose an AI-powered fitness app like **Fitbit**, **Apple Health**, or **Google Fit**. If you have a wearable device, sync it with the app.

2. **Step 2: Set a Daily Activity Goal**
   Set a goal for daily steps, exercise minutes, or calories burned. For example, aim to walk 6,000 steps or complete 30 minutes of light exercise.

3. **Step 3: Track Your Progress**
   Throughout the day, check your app to see how close you are to meeting your goal. Pay attention to any AI-generated reminders or suggestions to help you stay active.

Chapter 45: Maintaining Hobbies: Using AI for Gardening, Cooking

Hobbies are a great way to stay engaged and mentally active as you age, and AI can help you enjoy them even more. Whether you love **gardening, cooking, or crafting**, AI tools offer new ways to improve your skills, learn new techniques, and manage your hobbies more efficiently.

How AI Supports Your Hobbies

AI tools are available for a variety of hobbies, from gardening to cooking. Here's how AI enhances your favorite activities:

- **Gardening Help**: Apps like **PlantSnap** and **Garden Answers** use AI to identify plants, offer gardening tips, and track watering schedules. Simply take a picture of a plant, and AI will tell you what it is, how to care for it, and when to water it.

- **Cooking Assistance**: AI-powered apps like **Yummly** and **Tasty** offer personalized recipe suggestions based on your preferences, dietary needs, and what ingredients you have on hand. AI can even guide you through each step of the recipe, ensuring your meals turn out perfectly.

- **Crafting Ideas**: If you enjoy crafting or DIY projects, AI-powered platforms like **Pinterest** use your interests to recommend new projects or techniques. You can search for specific crafting ideas, and AI will suggest tutorials and inspiration based on what you like.

Example: Gardening with AI

Let's say you're unsure about how much water your houseplants need. You use the **PlantSnap** app to take a picture of each plant, and the AI identifies them and provides detailed care instructions. It even sets up a watering schedule for each plant, reminding you when it's time to water them based on their specific needs.

Why AI Hobbies Tools Are Helpful for Seniors

For seniors, AI offers a new way to enjoy hobbies by providing personalized guidance and suggestions. Whether you're learning how to cook new dishes, identifying plants in your garden, or finding new crafting ideas, AI helps you get the most out of your favorite activities.

Hands-On Exercise: Use AI to Enhance Your Hobbies

1. **Step 1: Choose a Hobby App**
   If you enjoy gardening, try **PlantSnap** or **Garden Answers**. For cooking, download **Yummly** or **Tasty**. If crafting is your thing, explore **Pinterest** for DIY project ideas.

2. **Step 2: Follow AI's Suggestions**
   Use the AI features to guide you. For example, let **PlantSnap** identify a plant and provide care instructions, or use **Yummly** to suggest a recipe based on what you have in your pantry.

3. **Step 3: Track Your Progress**
   Follow AI's recommendations and see how they improve your experience. For gardening, track how well your plants are doing with the suggested care, or follow a new recipe from start to finish and note how easy AI makes it.

Chapter 46: AI for Lifelong Learning: Courses, Skills, and Hobbies

AI is transforming **lifelong learning**, making it easier than ever for seniors to acquire new skills, learn new subjects, and stay intellectually engaged. Whether you want to take up a new hobby, learn a language, or explore an academic subject, AI-powered learning platforms offer personalized, flexible ways to continue learning throughout your life.

How AI Enhances Lifelong Learning

AI-powered platforms adapt to your pace, preferences, and learning style, offering courses, tutorials, and personalized learning paths. Here's how AI can support your learning journey:

- **Online Courses**: Platforms like **Coursera**, **Khan Academy**, and **edX** use AI to recommend courses based on your interests. You can learn about a wide range of subjects—from history to technology—and AI adjusts the content based on your progress and understanding.

- **Language Learning**: Apps like **Duolingo** and **Babbel** use AI to personalize language lessons. AI analyzes your strengths and weaknesses, offering extra practice on areas where you need improvement, making language learning more effective.

- **Skill Development**: AI can help you develop new skills like photography, art, or cooking. Websites like **Skillshare** use AI to recommend classes based on your interests, skill level, and learning history.

Example: Learning a New Skill with AI

Imagine you want to learn how to paint with watercolors. You join **Skillshare** and choose a beginner painting course. The AI tracks your progress and recommends follow-up lessons based on the techniques you've learned. You can go at your own pace, and AI suggests resources to help you improve along the way.

Why AI Lifelong Learning Tools Are Helpful for Seniors

For seniors, AI-powered learning platforms provide a flexible and engaging way to continue growing intellectually. Whether you're exploring a new hobby, brushing up on a skill, or learning something completely new, AI tailors the learning experience to your needs, ensuring you stay motivated and on track.

Hands-On Exercise: Explore AI Learning Tools

1. **Step 1: Choose a Learning Platform**
   Visit a platform like **Coursera**, **Khan Academy**, **Duolingo**, or **Skillshare** and explore the available courses or lessons.

2. **Step 2: Enroll in a Course or Lesson**
   Pick a subject or skill that interests you, such as a history course or a language lesson. Follow the AI's recommended learning path, and complete the first lesson.

3. **Step 3: Set a Learning Goal**
   Set a goal for your learning, such as completing one lesson per week.

Chapter 47: AI and Travel: Planning and Exploring with AI

Travel is one of life's greatest pleasures, and AI can make planning your trips and exploring new destinations easier than ever. From finding the best flight deals to offering personalized recommendations on what to do and see, AI-powered travel apps help you manage all aspects of your journey.

How AI Improves Travel Planning

AI helps streamline travel planning by providing real-time information and personalized suggestions based on your preferences. Here's how AI enhances your travel experience:

- **Finding Deals**: AI-powered apps like **Hopper** and **Skyscanner** help you find the best deals on flights and accommodations. They track prices over time and notify you when it's the right time to book, saving you money.
- **Personalized Itineraries**: AI apps like **TripIt** and **Google Travel** can automatically organize your travel itinerary based on your bookings. AI also suggests activities, tours, or restaurants based on your location and interests.
- **Language Assistance**: AI translation tools like **Google Translate** help you navigate foreign countries by translating signs, menus, and conversations in real-time. Just point your phone's camera at the text, and AI will instantly translate it.

Example: Using AI for a Vacation

Let's say you're planning a trip to Italy. You use **Hopper** to track flight prices, and AI notifies you when it's the best time to book. Once you've booked, **TripIt** organizes your itinerary, including your hotel reservations and day trips. During your trip, you use **Google Translate** to read a restaurant menu and order food in Italian, all with the help of AI.

Why AI Travel Tools Are Helpful for Seniors

For seniors, AI travel tools simplify the entire travel process, from booking flights and hotels to navigating new destinations. Whether you're planning a short weekend getaway or an international adventure, AI provides personalized suggestions and real-time assistance, ensuring a smooth and stress-free experience.

Hands-On Exercise: Plan a Trip with AI

1. **Step 1: Download a Travel App**
   Download an AI-powered travel app like **Hopper** or **Skyscanner** and start searching for flights or hotel deals.

2. **Step 2: Use AI to Plan Your Itinerary**
   Use an app like **TripIt** or **Google Travel** to organize your trip. Enter your travel dates, and let AI suggest activities or places to visit based on your preferences.

3. **Step 3: Use a Translation Tool**
   If you're traveling to a non-English-speaking country, try **Google Translate**. Take a picture of a sign, menu, or text in another language and let AI translate it for you.

Chapter 48: AI for Reading: Audiobooks, E-books, and Personalized Suggestions

Reading is a favorite pastime for many seniors, and AI can make reading even more enjoyable and accessible through **audiobooks**, **e-books**, and personalized reading recommendations. Whether you prefer listening to books or reading on a tablet, AI-powered apps offer easy ways to discover new titles and enjoy your favorite genres.

How AI Enhances the Reading Experience

AI can recommend books, customize your reading experience, and even read to you. Here's how AI makes reading more enjoyable:

- **Audiobooks**: Apps like **Audible** use AI to recommend audiobooks based on your listening habits. You can download and listen to books anytime, making reading more accessible, especially for those with vision impairments.

- **E-books**: AI-powered e-book platforms like **Kindle** or **Google Books** offer personalized recommendations based on your reading history. You can also adjust text size, font, and brightness to make reading more comfortable.

- **Personalized Book Suggestions**: AI apps like **Goodreads** analyze your reading preferences and suggest books you're likely to enjoy. If you rate a book you loved, AI will recommend similar titles from the same genre or author.

Example: Discovering New Books with AI

Imagine you've just finished a historical novel on **Kindle**. AI suggests another book by the same author or in the same genre, saving you time searching for your next great read. If you're using **Audible**, AI recommends a new audiobook based on your past listens, making it easy to stay immersed in the world of books.

Why AI Reading Tools Are Helpful for Seniors

For seniors, AI reading tools provide more ways to enjoy books, whether through audiobooks or e-books. Personalized suggestions save time, while audiobook options offer a way to enjoy books without straining your eyes.

Hands-On Exercise: Explore AI Reading Tools

1. **Step 1: Download an E-book or Audiobook App**
   Try **Kindle**, **Google Books**, or **Audible**. Explore the book recommendations based on your past reading or listening habits.

2. **Step 2: Start a New Book**
   Choose a recommended e-book or audiobook and start reading or listening. Adjust the font size or audio speed if needed to make the experience more comfortable.

3. **Step 3: Rate the Book**
   After finishing a book, rate it in the app. Let AI use your rating to recommend your next book based on your pref

Chapter 49: Staying Safe Online: AI for Cybersecurity and Fraud Prevention

Staying safe online is essential, especially as cyber threats and scams become more sophisticated. Fortunately, AI can help protect your online privacy and prevent fraud by identifying suspicious activities, securing your devices, and safeguarding your personal information. For seniors, AI-powered cybersecurity tools offer peace of mind while navigating the internet.

How AI Enhances Cybersecurity

AI tools are constantly monitoring online activities to protect your data from hackers and scammers. Here's how AI improves your online safety:

- **Fraud Detection**: Banks and financial institutions use AI to detect fraudulent activity. If AI detects unusual spending patterns, it will alert you and block suspicious transactions.

- **Password Security**: AI-powered password managers like **LastPass** and **Dashlane** help you create and store strong, unique passwords for your online accounts. AI also ensures your passwords are encrypted, making them more difficult to hack.

- **Phishing Protection**: AI tools like **Google Safe Browsing** scan websites for potential threats and warn you if you're about to visit a suspicious or malicious site. Many email providers use AI to identify phishing emails and filter them out before they reach your inbox.

Example: Avoiding an Online Scam

Imagine you receive an email that looks like it's from your bank, asking you to click a link and verify your account information. **Gmail's** AI detects that the email is likely a phishing attempt and moves it to your spam folder, preventing you from falling for the scam.

Why AI Cybersecurity Tools Are Helpful for Seniors

For seniors, AI-powered cybersecurity tools provide an extra layer of protection against scams, hacking, and fraud. These tools automatically secure your online accounts and alert you to suspicious activity, making it easier to stay safe while browsing or shopping online.

Hands-On Exercise: Strengthen Your Online Security with AI

1. **Step 1: Install a Password Manager**
   Download **LastPass** or **Dashlane** and set up a secure account. Let AI generate and store strong passwords for your online accounts.

2. **Step 2: Review Your Email's Spam Folder**
   Open your email and check the spam folder. Look for any phishing emails or suspicious messages that AI has filtered out for you.

3. **Step 3: Enable Security Alerts**
   Enable fraud detection alerts for your bank or credit card accounts. Let AI notify you of any unusual activity and review your transactions regularly.

Chapter 50: The Future of AI: What's Next for Seniors?

As AI continues to evolve, its potential to improve the lives of seniors grows as well. From healthcare advancements to smarter home devices and even more personalized services, the future of AI promises even greater accessibility, convenience, and independence for older adults.

How AI Will Continue to Improve Senior Life

Here's what seniors can expect from AI in the near future:

- **Healthcare Innovations**: AI will play a larger role in healthcare, offering more sophisticated remote monitoring, disease prediction, and personalized treatments. Wearable devices will continue to evolve, providing even better health data and real-time alerts for potential issues.

- **More Personalized AI Companions**: AI companions like **Elliq** and **Replika** will become even more interactive, offering deeper conversations and more tailored support. These companions may soon be able to detect emotions and respond empathetically, making them more effective at providing social and emotional support.

- **Increased Accessibility**: AI will continue to improve accessibility tools for seniors, from voice-controlled devices to smart homes. As technology becomes more integrated into everyday life, AI will help seniors maintain their independence by automating tasks and providing easy-to-use interfaces for everything from cooking to managing medications.

The Role of Seniors in Shaping AI's Future

Seniors are not just passive users of AI technology—they are key to shaping its future. As AI becomes more widespread, feedback from older adults will help developers create tools that meet the unique needs of seniors. Your experience with AI tools today helps drive innovation and improve technology for future generations.

Hands-On Exercise: Stay Informed About AI Developments

1. **Step 1: Follow AI News**
   Stay up to date on AI advancements by following tech news websites, like **Wired** or **TechCrunch**, or watching tech-related news segments on TV.

2. **Step 2: Test New AI Tools**
   When new AI tools or features are released, take time to explore them. Whether it's a new healthcare app or a smart home feature, your feedback can help shape the future of AI.

3. **Step 3: Share Your Experience**
   Share your thoughts and experiences with AI through online forums, surveys, or by discussing them with friends and family. Your insights are valuable in helping improve AI tools for everyone.

Don't miss out!

Visit the website below and you can sign up to receive emails whenever Josiah Wolff publishes a new book. There's no charge and no obligation.

https://books2read.com/r/B-A-YXGMC-WVLAF

BOOKS 2 READ

Connecting independent readers to independent writers.

www.ingramcontent.com/pod-product-compliance
Lightning Source LLC
Chambersburg PA
CBHW051211160726
47994CB00002B/559